COLLECTOR'S GUIDE TO
BASEBALL
MEMORABILIA

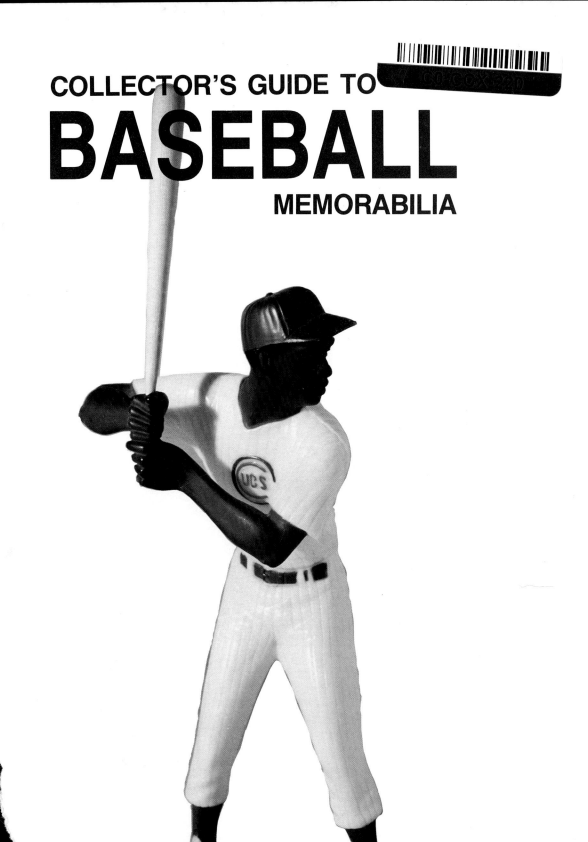

COLLECTOR'S GUIDE TO
BASEBALL
MEMORABILIA

Don Raycraft
Stew Salowitz

COLLECTOR BOOKS
A Division of Schroeder Publishing Co., Inc.

The current values in this book should be used only as a guide. They are not intended to set prices, which vary from one section of the country to another. Auction prices as well as dealer prices vary greatly and are affected by condition as well as demand. Neither the Author nor the Publisher assumes responsibility for any losses that might be incurred as a result of consulting this guide.

Additional copies of this book may be ordered from:

Collector Books
P.O. Box 3009
Paducah, KY 42001

@$14.95 Add $1.00 for postage and handling.

Copyright: Don Raycraft, Stew Salowitz, 1987

Dedicated to Dorcas Salowitz, Emma Lou Raycraft and mothers everywhere who never quite understood, but always found an extra nickel for that pack of gum cards.

Acknowledgments

A book of this type is impossible to do without the assistance of a diverse group of individuals from across the nation. The authors are indebted to the following:

Barry Halper, Robert Stephen Simon, Bill Henderson, Dick Dobbins, Bill Colby, Denny Matthews, Senator Alex Hood, Ron Martin, Craig Holly, Steve Epperson, Frank McNeny, Scott, Mike and Craig Raycraft, R. Scott Robbins, Willis E. Kern, Jr., Lanny Lobdell, Andy Fedder, Rusty Petty, Debbie and Billy Salowitz, Gordon Hodges, Matt Deneen, Royal J. Norman, Miles Bertsche, John and Jamie Whitlow, Jim Clark, Todd Smith, Jim and Marybeth Doherty, Dave Flyipek, Ronn Buhrow, Ryan Tucker, Mike and Matt Bazzani, Steve Quertermous, Bill Schroeder, Rob and Eric Vogel, Jonathan Laughlin, Diana Wollenberg-Nelson, Cory Roop, Huey Lewis, Justin Kern, Thomas Krones, Erland Bergen, Andrew Tucker, Marty Capodice, Don Munson, and Peter Delsignore.

Photography

Jon Balke
Mike Raycraft
Dick Dobbins
Ralph Bernays
Craig Holly
Carol Raycraft
The cover photograph was taken by Jon Balke.

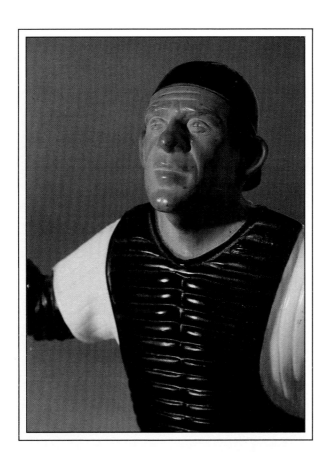

Foreword

By Denny Matthews

(Denny Matthews, one of major league baseball's most accomplished and respected play-by-play announcers, has broadcast Kansas City Royals games since the club's inception in 1969. Matthews was born and raised in Bloomington-Normal, Illinois and played baseball and football at Illinois Wesleyan University.)

It seems to me that everyone collects or saves some thing or things. Do you know anyone who doesn't?

My own collecting "career" started in the spring of 1952 when my father, George, came home from work one evening and handed me a package of baseball cards. I'll never forget the first player to come out of that pack: Robin Roberts, card number 59.

So my interest, and my collection, grew. A pocketful of baseball cards turned out to be quite versatile. You could take them to school and make trades with the kids who didn't know too much about the players yet, and get all the Cardinals and Cubs players you needed. You would always keep a few of your favorites in your shirt pocket, and when things would get a little slow in the schoolroom in the middle of a warm spring afternoon, you could sneak a peek at a couple of cards, read the player facts on the back, and daydream about the ballgame that would start at Fell Avenue Park shortly after the three o'clock dismissal bell.

You could use the cards while listening to a ballgame, making sure the cards were placed in the proper batting order as the players came up for their turn. You could use the cards to complement any number of table-top or pinball types of games played in the cool shade of a front porch. You could even put the cards under your pillow at night, or just sit and idly shuffle, shuffle, shuffle them . . . they just felt so good in your hands.

Some people are not exposed to, or don't get interested in, baseball cards until they are adults. I could try to explain to them what they have missed, but they wouldn't understand. As much, or perhaps more, as a song from long ago will recall a memory, a single baseball card can unleash a flood of flashbacks. All of them are pleasant.

I guess that's why I've kept my baseball cards for all these years - we grew up together. We shared dreams then. We share memories now.

Denny Matthews, broadcaster for the Kansas City Royals.

Introduction

By Don Raycraft

In the early Fifties, my parents and I went to Florida for two weeks each winter. In addition to my spelling book and school assignment sheet, I annually took along my Walt Dropo first baseman's glove and a shoe box filled with baseball cards.

My father was a Yankees fan and we saw as many spring training games as possible. He also thought that his only son would be a "bonus baby" and eventually would sign with the Bronx Bombers. He was positive that I had as much talent as Frank Leja, who was being touted as the next Lou Gehrig. My father was absolutely correct about the similar skills of Frank Leja and me. Neither of us made it.

My father encouraged me to go up to Bauer, Mantle, Berra, Martin, Reynolds, Lopat and Stengel and stand in short lines for autographs. I never did. However, my own children have become the collectors their grandfather had wanted. The hesitation that bedeviled their father in securing an autograph presents no problem for them.

I read *Sport Magazine*, cut out the full-page color pictures and nailed them to a plaster wall in my room. My mother has never forgiven me.

The highlight of my childhood collecting career occurred when an older boy from down the block traded me "a ball that Jim Rivera fouled off" for 385 Topps cards from the 1953 season. When he came home from work that night, my father pointed out to me that American League teams did not normally buy their baseballs at Montgomery Ward.

The gentleman who took many of the photos in this book was given a set of 1951 Bowman cards when he was a child. He liked them so much, he decided to take a paper punch and put holes in the corners of the cards of his favorite players. He liked Willie Mays and Ted Williams; he didn't pay any attention to Eddie Joost. He still has the cards and two sons who will profit from his misspent youth. He lost the paper punch a long time ago.

Introduction

By Stew Salowitz

Like every red-blooded American boy, I collected baseball cards. A hopeless Giants fan, I sought (either by purchasing or trading) to have every Giants player many times over, sometimes squandering valuable Cardinals or Cubs to neighborhood pals for just one more Jim Ray Hart card.

Sometime between the age at which I would hook my ballglove on my bike handlebars and the age I discovered girls and cars, my baseball cards were dispatched. Some were used in a garage sale. Some were given to younger kids. Many were thrown away. Only the 1962 Topps set remains and those cards are glued tightly in a scrapbook!

There are countless "horror" stories like this of baseball collectibles being discarded or misused. Fortunately, however, there are ways to resurrect the past. These days you can buy anything from jerseys and bats to cards and yearbooks. From Hartland statues to bobbin' head dolls. Thanks to the many shows now staged across the country, you are also able to obtain (for a fee) that autograph you've been coveting for years.

In this book you'll see various aspects of baseball collectibles. You'll see things that are readily available and you'll see items that are legitimately priceless. There will be the obvious and the obscure.

If you finish looking at the pictures and reading the interesting oral histories that are in this book and find yourself asking this question, "Why would anybody want to collect something like that?", then you obviously have no sense of the great and fascinating history of baseball. You have my sympathy.

People collect stamps, coins, butterflies, books, records, antiques, paperweights, Hummel figurines, art and any number of other things. In collecting baseball memorabilia, people are surrounding themselves with history - with at bats, hits, runs, errors, diving catches, chewing tobacco, bubble gum and illustrious characters who played the game for our enjoyment.

It is for your enjoyment that we offer this work.

Baseball Cards

In recent years due to the work of Dr. James Beckett, *Sports Collectors Digest, Baseball Cards Magazine, Baseball Hobby News, Baseball Card News*, and several other equally informative publications, collectors of baseball cards can be kept in constant contact with the monetary values of their cardboard treasures.

Most of us did not have this luxury when we were children. We thought in terms of a Snider, two Hodges, and a Repulski for a Mantle. Kids didn't buy cards from dealers by the set, they stood in line at the corner Piggly Wiggly with a nickel and a pounding pulse in hopes of finding a Mays or Jackie Robinson. The majority of us walked away with a Dee Fondy or a Curt Raydon.

Major league broadcaster Denny Matthews, legendary collector Barry Halper, card dealer Bill Henderson and the authors all point out how their interest in cards initially fueled their love of baseball and resulted in a lifelong obsession with the game.

This slim volume could not begin to provide the values or history of baseball cards. That task is being capably accomplished by the several publications listed above. Our primary intent is to provide some insight into the vast array of baseball memoribilia that is available to collectors today.

1953 Topps gum cards worth about $10.00 to $20.00 each in excellent to mint condition with the exception of Berra ($20.00-$40.00) and Mantle ($125.00-375.00). Baseball card pricing depends on condition, rarity, and popularity of the ballplayer.

Collector's Chronology

1877   Spaulding Company distributes a baseball guide.

1887   Old Judge and Gypsy Queen cigarettes have photographs of baseball players included in their packages.

1910   Honus Wagner is furious when his picture is included in a package of Sweet Caporal cigarettes and his card is withdrawn.

1933   Goudey Big League Gum produces a baseball card set with 240 players.

1953   Hartland Plastics Company of Hartland, Wisconsin begins production of 8″ baseball figures.

1963   Hartland ceases production of baseball figures. Eighteen different major league players were depicted in individual statues that sold for $3.00-5.00 each.

1964   Curtelch Company begins to issue yellow Hall of Fame "plaques" or postcards.

1977   Gateway Stamp Company issues its first baseball commemorative envelopes in honor of Lou Brock tying and breaking the career stolen base record of Ty Cobb in San Diego on August 29.

1980   Perez-Steele Galleries offers the first three series of limited edition Hall of Fame postcards.

1980   The First National Baseball Card Sports Collector Convention is held in Los Angeles.

1982   Donruss releases first 26 Diamond Kings

Barry Halper

(Barry Halper is the chief executive officer of the Halper Brothers, Inc., a paper company in Elizabeth, NJ. He is a partner in the New York Yankees and undoubtedly the world's foremost collector of baseball memorabilia. His collection runs the gamut from World Series programs and press pins to Mickey Mantle uniforms.)

I was born in Newark, New Jersey and in about 1948 (when I was eight years old) I went into the candy store one day and saw these black and white Bowman baseball cards for sale. At that time the set consisted of 48 cards, and after stops at that store day after day, I wound up with about six sets. I'd flip them and trade them with other kids.

One thing about those days was that my school was right around the corner from my house. There was no bussing, everybody would walk to school. You had a session in the morning, came home for lunch, then went back to school. We had about 45 minutes for lunch and probably half of that time was spent in the candy store going through newspapers, checking on how the Giants, Dodgers, and Yankees were all doing. Plus we had the Newark Bears and the Jersey City Giants all within a 20-mile radius. Everybody was always baseball crazy. Professional football hadn't hit its peak, professional basketball was in its infant stages, nobody cared about hockey and soccer wasn't even born in the United States.

In 1949, Bowman came out with a color set of cards and I used to take these down to Ruppert Stadium, the home of the Newark Bears (then an affiliate of the Yankees), to get them signed. It wasn't like today's minor leagues where it's all kids coming up. In those days you had a lot of major leaguers who had finished their careers and were trying to hang on and earn some money playing in the minors.

By hanging around the clubhouse, getting guys to sign things and running all around collecting Newark Bears programs, I became a nuisance to a player named Lou Novikoff (who was called "The Mad Russian"). Every day when I saw him I'd ask him to sign my program and he'd say, "Geez, again? How many times am I going to sign that for you?" He said, "I have an idea. You be here tomorrow and I'll bring something for you, IF you promise not to ask me for any more autographs." I said, "Okay, Mr. Novikoff," and he said, "Just call me 'The Russian'. I'm 'The Mad Russian'." I'll never forget those words. The next day he brought me a bag containing a uniform that once belonged to Barney McCosky (a player in the Thirties and Forties). That happened in 1948 and I still have that uniform. By the time I was in high school I had 75 uniforms.

I now lack just eight of having every Hall of Famer's uniform. That, naturally, doesn't include those who wouldn't have uniforms because they were elected due to meritorious service. I have a lot of duplicate uniforms, too. I have Casey Stengel uniforms from when he was with Boston, Brooklyn and from when he managed the Yankees. I've done all this through diligent letter-writing, tracing down players and what happened to their families. It's hard work but it has it rewards.

Which uniform in my collection is my favorite? It depends on what day you ask me. The autographed Ty Cobb Philadelphia A's uniform is great. There's Babe Ruth's first uniform with the Red Sox in 1914, and Joe DiMaggio's San Francisco Seals jersey. But I really believe the Lou Gehrig autographed uniform is my favorite. Someone who was obviously ahead of his time had Gehrig sign the jersey in 1936.

I have quite a few Babe Ruth contracts, his 1925 divorce papers, his Last Will and Testament and the correspondence leading up to Ruth's sale to the Yankees from the Red Sox - all obtained from a box of papers that once belonged to former Yankees owner Jacob Ruppert. I got these from a guy who lived in a house once owned by Ruppert. They were in a shoebox in the attic. I also have Ruth's personal spittoon engraved with the initials "GHR", a lock of Ruth's hair with a letter of authenticity, over 100 Babe Ruth autographed baseballs and four of Ruth's uniforms when he was with the Yankees.

I have Babe's glove that he wore in the 1921 season, back in the days when players would just leave their gloves on the field when they went in to bat. In an exhibition game at Ebbets Field, Ruth was playing rightfield, but didn't come out for the ninth inning. After the game, this kid ran out onto the field and grabbed the glove, knowing it was Ruth's, and stuffed it under his shirt. Babe charged out of the dugout yelling, "Hey, sonny, get back here!" Well, the kid stopped, because it was Babe Ruth calling him, and went back to return the glove to Ruth. Ruth told the boy he could have the glove, but the kid never used it because he was righthanded and the glove was for a lefty. After many, many years of having the glove sit in a box, the owner got in touch with me and we made a deal for Babe Ruth's glove.

I always like to have a type of theme in my collecting. For instance, I had Cy Young sign a ball for me in 1954 and I've proceeded to get every Cy Young Award winner on that ball except two - Mike McCormick and Mike Marshall. Another example is when I was having Pete Rose sign some baseballs, he signed one that Joe DiMaggio had already autographed. It never dawned on me, but Pete said, "There you go. Now you have a baseball signed by the two guys who have the game's longest batting streaks." Then I thought it out and had Pete sign a ball that was autographed by Ty Cobb.

Collecting today is so different because we have so many baseball card shows across the country where ballplayers will autograph items for money. You can probably get anybody who's anybody if you go to these shows. But it's difficult to go to a hotel and get a big name star to sign things for you, much more difficult than it was in my early days in the late Forties and the Fifties. I'd suggest people try to collect as much as they can, then do some trading. The most important thing is to really want to do it. Be creative, develop some themes of your own for your collecting, like getting a ball signed by guys who have pitched no-hitters or guys who have hit over 300 or 400 home runs.

Why did I get so involved in baseball? Why not, say, basketball? In basketball, what can you collect except a ball and ten different uniforms or sneakers? There are no artifacts, no gloves, no spikes. Baseball has such a history statistically. Can anyone tell you what Wilt Chamberlain's foul shooting percentage was or what Joe Namath's passing percentage was? No, but you ask them about Ty Cobb's batting average or about Pete Rose or Hank Aaron or Babe Ruth and his home runs. Kids know about baseball. My ten year old son, Jason, has the advantage of seeing all my baseball stuff and he knows about players who were dead long before he was born.

Somewhere along the line it's as if some abstract quantity grabbed me and said, "Hey! I'm baseball! Follow me!" I've come in contact with a lot of nice people, people willing to help each other out. Overall, collecting baseball memorabilia has been very rewarding to me. I always treat it as having therapy - seeing this historical collection is something I look forward to and is theraputic. A hobby is a great thing, whether it's collecting baseball or record albums or stamps.

Barry Halper, flanked by his son, Jason (on his right), and Todd Murcer, has amassed the nation's premiere private collection of baseball memorabilia.

Former Cardinal great Stan Musial is one of many baseball standouts who has visited the Halper collection.

Halper and home run king Henry Aaron.

At Halper's New Jersey home, Pete Rose displays Ty Cobb's Tigers uniform and the smoking jacket of the former all-time hit leader. The left breast pocket of the silk-lined jacket carries a crossed bat logo and Cobb's initials.

The Puffed Wheat advertisement featuring Babe Ruth is an example of the many advertising pieces in the Halper collection. The bust is of Connie Mack, who in 53 years as a major league manager was on the winning end of 3,776 games.

Halper, a partner in the New York Yankees ownership, has been collecting baseball memorabilia since his grade school days in the late 1940s.

Joe DiMaggio's rookie uniform with the New York Yankees is part of the Halper collection. DiMaggio made his debut with the Yanks in 1936 and was elected to the Hall of Fame in 1955. He had a lifetime batting mark of .325 with 361 home runs in his 13 season career.

Autographed Baseballs

Hall of Famer Clark Griffith personalized this ball for Bloomington, Illinois sports editor Fred "Brick" Young in 1942. Personalized baseballs tend to appreciate at a lesser rate than those balls which are merely signed.

A 1983 50th anniversary All-Star Game baseball with the printed signature of baseball commissioner Bowie Kuhn. All-Star Game and World Series balls carry the signature of the commissioner rather than the individual league presidents.

A game ball from the 1984 Summer Olympics, made to major league specifications by Rawlings.

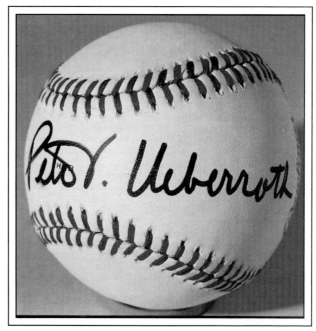

A 1984 Olympic Games baseball, signed by Peter Ueberroth.

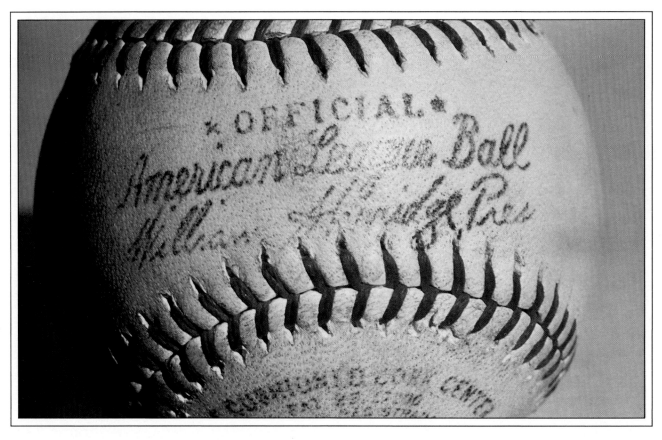

A 1942 American League baseball with the printed signature of then-league president Will Harridge.

Baseball signed by Hall of Famers Hoyt Wilhelm, Buck Leonard and Yogi Berra. This ball was signed in Cooperstown on the day of Wilhelm's induction in 1985.

Hall of Famers Enos Slaughter, Ralph Kiner and Lou Brock.

Henry Aaron was inducted into baseball's Hall of Fame in 1982.

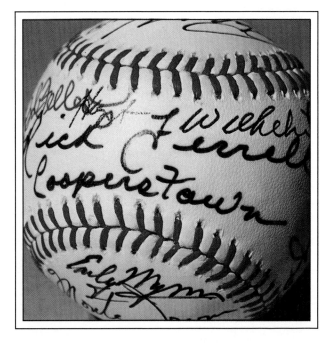

Hall of Famers Bill Terry, Luis Aparicio and Monte Irvin. Autographs of Latin American players are generally more difficult to obtain, simply because of geography. This Aparicio signature was obtained at a show in Chicago in 1985.

Rick Ferrell was inducted into the Hall of Fame in 1984 as a player. Ferrell appeared in 1,884 games in 18 seasons.

New York Yankees great Edward "Whitey" Ford, winner of 25 games in 1961, retired in 1967 with a total of 236 career victories.

Jack Roosevelt Robinson was elected to the Hall of Fame in 1962. Signed Robinson baseballs are uncommon.

An official Hall of Fame baseball signed and dated by Cardinals great Bob Gibson.

Elected to the Hall in 1974, Mickey Mantle is among the most popular players in the game's history and is a great attraction at national card and memorabilia shows.

This bat commemorating Willie Mays's 600th career home run was presented to selected sporting goods dealers by the Adirondack company.

Baltimore Orioles shortstop Cal Ripken, Jr.

This baseball was signed by St. Louis Cardinals shortstop Ozzie Smith at a Cardinal Caravan visit to Bloomington, Illinois. Winter "caravans", conducted by most major league teams, provide fans a great opportunity to obtain autographs.

Roger Maris put an asterisk in the record books in 1961 when he broke Babe Ruth's record for home runs in a season.

St. Louis Cardinals speedster Vince Coleman.

A Boston Red Sox autographed baseball, circa 1966, featuring the signature of Carl Yastrzemski in the "sweet spot".

An official Pacific Coast League baseball signed by members of the Phoenix Giants, circa 1981.

A cinch for baseball's Hall of Fame, Pete Rose set the mark for most hits in a career on September 11, 1985.

Some collectors specialize in particular players or teams. The hat, batting gloves and wrist band were game worn by Chili Davis, outfielder with the San Francisco Giants.

This 1948 National League baseball was discovered in the basement of a rural New Hamsphire sporting goods store. The ball was still sealed in its original Spalding box.

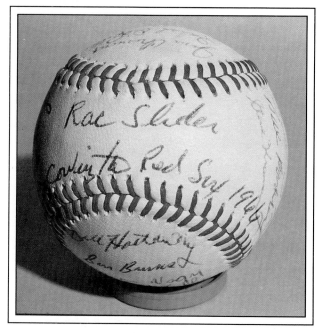

An inexpensive and easily acquired collection of autographed baseballs can begin with local minor league teams, such as this ball signed by the Covington (Virginia) Red Sox in 1966.

A 1985 Erie Cardinals autographed baseball from the New York-Penn League.

The upper row consists of two pre-1900 baseballs. The ball at the lower left is dated 1885 and was machine-stitched. This can be compared with the modern day ball. In the 19th century it was not uncommon for a professional game to be played with less than three balls.

Bill Colby

(Bill Colby is the proprietor of Kenrich Company, a business that deals in the sale of major league baseball bats of various kinds. Kenrich Company also sells baseball cards, comics, paper collectibles, post cards, stamps, autographs and old newspapers. Kenrich Company is located at 9418-S Las Tunas Drive, Temple City, California 91780.)

One of my baseball card customers turned out to be a property man with one of the local baseball clubs, and he told me he had some bats that had been discarded by the team after the bats had been cracked. He asked if I wanted to buy them, and I took about 20 of them as something different to sell. Well, they sold right away and then I bought more from him and the first thing I knew, that part of my business started growing.

The bats I get come from teams, from people who work in the clubhouses, equipment managers, people who know the bat boys, or the bat boys themselves. I got a bat once from a bat boy who called me from a game that was still in progress, wanting to know if I wanted to buy the Mizuno bat of a very prominent player whose name sounds like a flower. I agreed on the price and it came right from the game.

People buy bats for different reasons - some people buy them because they happen to have the same name as the ballplayer on the bat. Some people collect team bats, others try to obtain their favorite players. A granddaughter of an old-time player contacted me in search of a bat of his. She said the family had everything else connected with him when he played ball, but they didn't have a bat and they were thrilled to get one.

It goes without saying that collectors should buy from someone who's reliable or somebody they know. A person might not be able to say exactly what game a bat was used in, but you can tell if a bat is authentic by looking at the bat's knob. If it's a Louisville Slugger and it has a number embedded on the knob (33, 34 or 35), that is the length of the bat and that designates a store model bat. Also, store-bought bats will say "Flame Tempered" on them; major league bats will say "Powerized". Adirondack bats will have the model number on the knob, not the size of the bat.

I think that game-used, uncracked, cracked or even piece-missing bats are more valuable than a mint bat. Mint bats can sometimes be ordered from a company and therefore they are more plentiful. A game-used bat is positive evidence that it was a part of an actual game, not just factory ordered. Game-used bats are usually more expensive than mint bats.

Ted Williams and Jackie Robinson bats have been mass-produced so often that it's easy to find a store-bought bat of theirs, but their authentic, game-used bats are rare, scarce and high-priced. Somebody at Hillerich & Bradsby (manufacturers of Louisville Sluggers) told me once that in the pre-1950s or pre-1960s days, players might use a store-model bat. So you can't say positively that a store-model bat was not used in a game. But those old bats are pretty hard to obtain.

Here at Kenrich Company, we've had bats from Honus Wagner, Lou Gehrig, and some from Babe Ruth come through to our company. A local television newscaster came and did a story that showed him swinging that original Ruth bat, which I finally sold for around $900. The Gehrig model sold for $1,100.

These days, Don Mattingly, Daryl Strawberry, Cal Ripken, Jr., Wade Boggs and Dwight Gooden have been hot selling bats. Of course, they're harder for me to obtain, too. I have to wait for somebody to refer a bat to me. I can't just go out and order the potentially big sellers. At Kenrich Company, we price our bats because of supply and demand. Guys like those I've mentioned, along with Rickey Henderson and Reggie Jackson, I can barely keep in stock. Obviously, from a business standpoint, popular players will fetch higher prices.

The way I understand it, the ballclubs own the bats. They buy them at a cost of around $12 or $13 apiece for the players. But the players can order them, too, if they're doing a show or something. They have their agent call, order the bats, then use them at a show to sell along with their autographs.

As in all collectibles, a person should buy what he likes and should remember that it's a hobby and it's for fun, instead of just something for investment. Investments will go up in price and they'll go down in price. If a person wants to own a game-used baseball bat of a certain player, they shouldn't worry if they paid too much . . . they should want to own it for fun and because it gives them pleasure. Having a bat is a unique thing - it'll never rot or deteriorate or get ruined, unless in a fire. It's a good collectible.

At Kenrich, bats are labelled
with each player's name, then
boxed and stored.

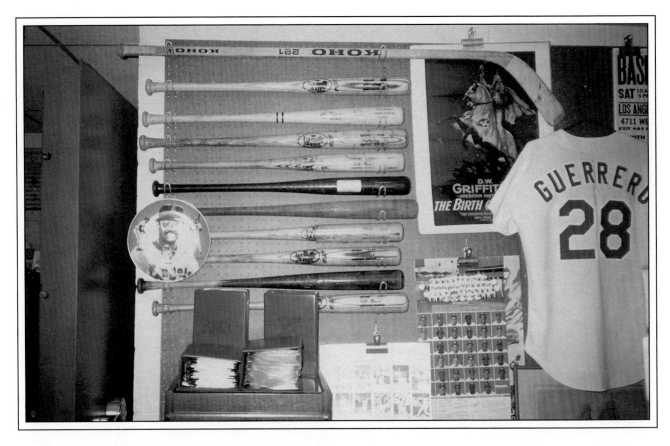

Bill Colby's Kenrich Company is the largest source of game-used bats for collectors.

The upper bat is from the 1880's; the middle bat is also a pre-1900 bat with an unusual rounded handle; the bottom bat is a contemporary example with a thin handle preferred by most players.

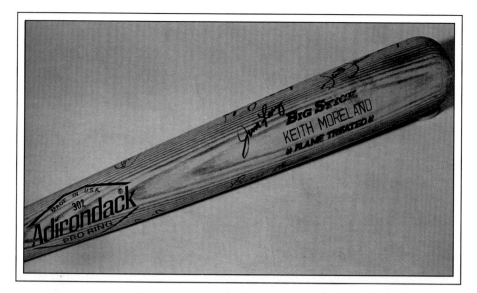

An Adironback bat, game-used by
Keith Moreland.

A bat provided by the St. Louis
Cardinals to their minor league af-
filiates for the 1985 season.

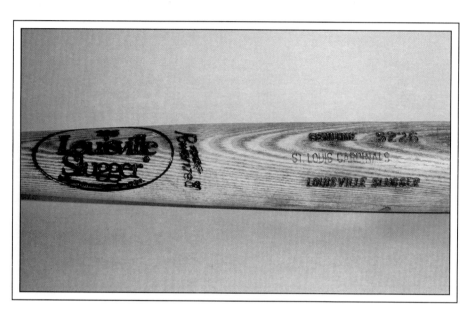

Bats made for pitchers (like this one
for Dave LaPoint) are less common
than bats produced for everyday
position players.

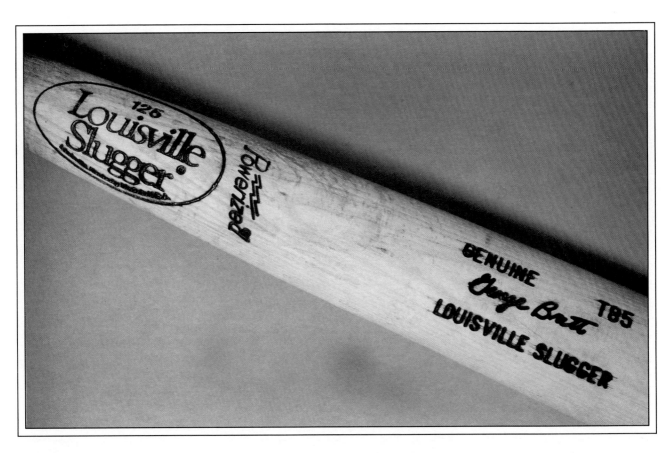

George Brett of the Kansas City Royals is one of only a handful of big league players who uses a bat without a varnished finish.

On a bat made for major league players, the knob is free of the numeric markings indicating bat size. The ''GB-5'' stands for George Brett and his uniform number.

Game-used bats by superstars (such as Mike Schmidt) can cost collectors as much as $150.

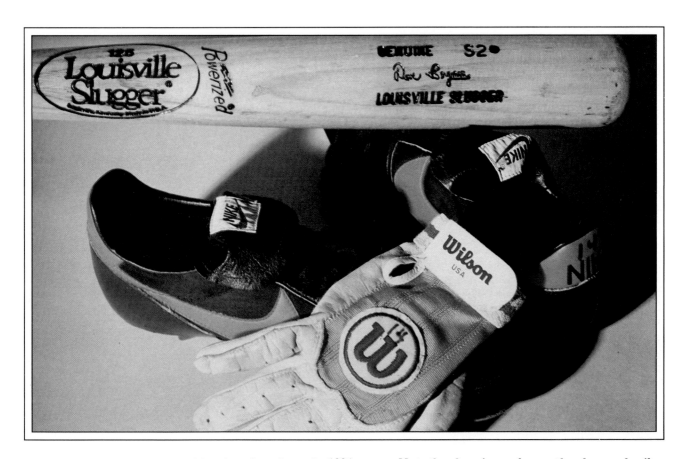

Dave Bergman's bat, spikes and batting glove from the 1984 season. Note the player's number on the glove and spikes.

A 1980 World Series bat, issued to Phillies players.

An impressed autograph of Pete Rose on a 1980 World Series bat.

The Cooperstown Bat Company is one of the few small operations still hand-turning baseball bats.

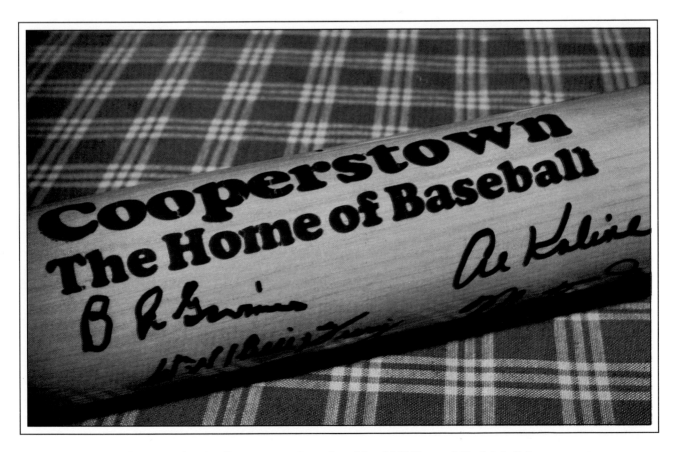

An example of a Cooperstown bat, signed by Al Kaline and Burleigh Grimes.

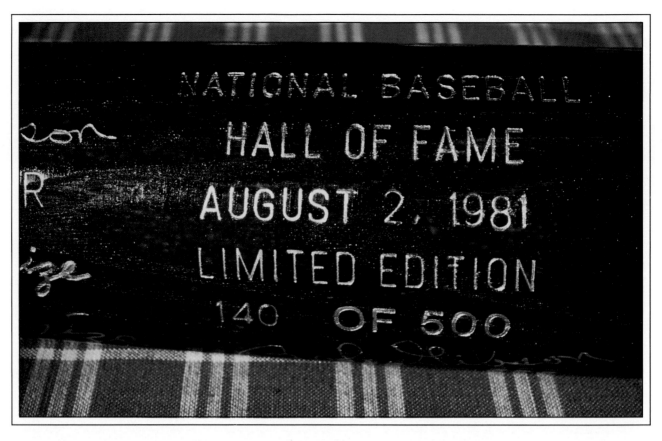

A bat, issued in a limited edition of 500 and sold by the Hall of Fame, commemorates each year's induction.

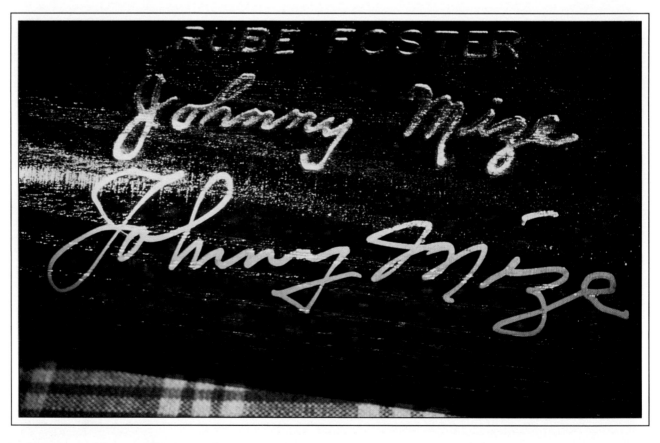

The signature of Johnny Mize in metallic pen on a Hall of Fame bat. The bats were initially priced in the $25.00-35.00 range, but have appreciated in value each year.

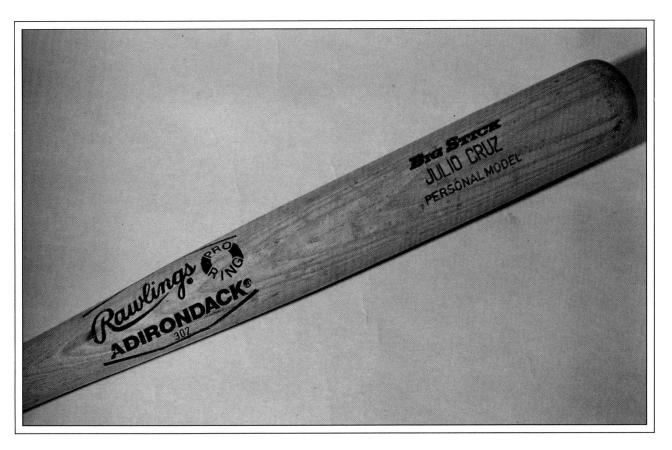

The bats of players who do not qualify as "stars" can be purchased for $10.00-20.00.

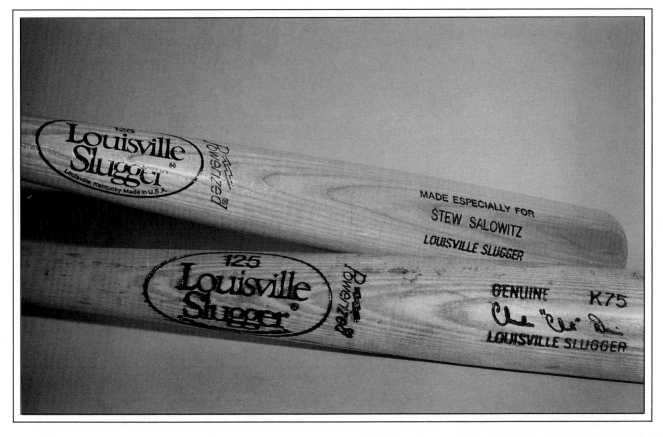

The Louisville Slugger Company has made personalized bats available to the general public. Note that the Salowitz bat does not carry an impressed signature as does the bat made for Chili Davis. It is important that collectors become aware of the various markings on professional bats.

An autographed pair of Nike baseball spikes worn by future Hall of Famer Mike Schmidt. Spikes, like hats, batting gloves and wrist bands normally carry the individual player's number.

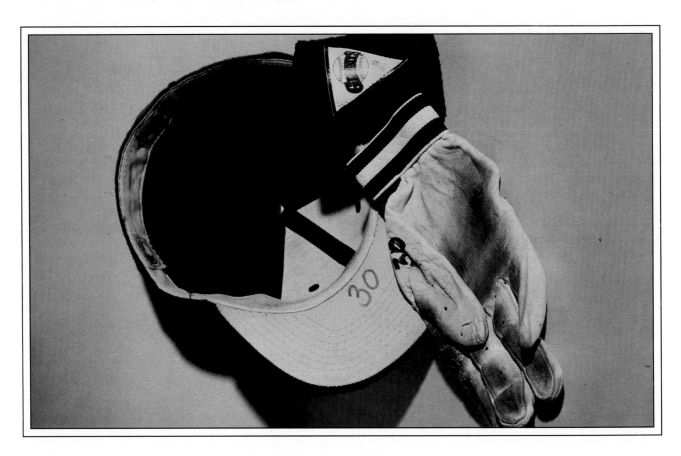

Another example of numbered gear.

Batting glove of utility infielder-outfielder Dave Bergman. During the winter months, many players donate equipment to charity auctions. This provides collectors a chance to secure items at potentially reasonable prices.

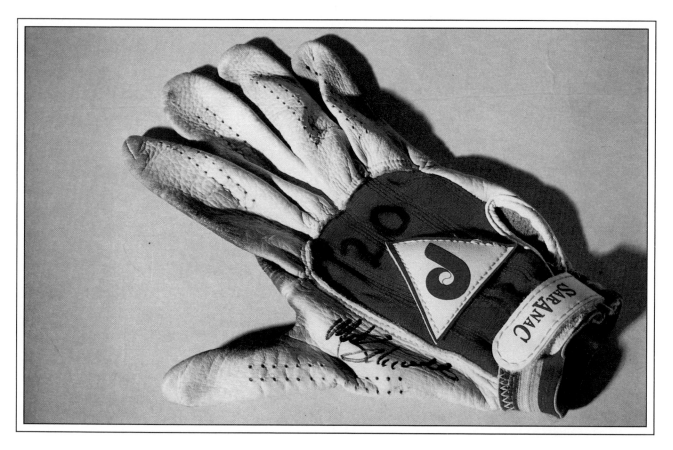

Game-used batting glove of Philadelphia's Mike Schmidt.

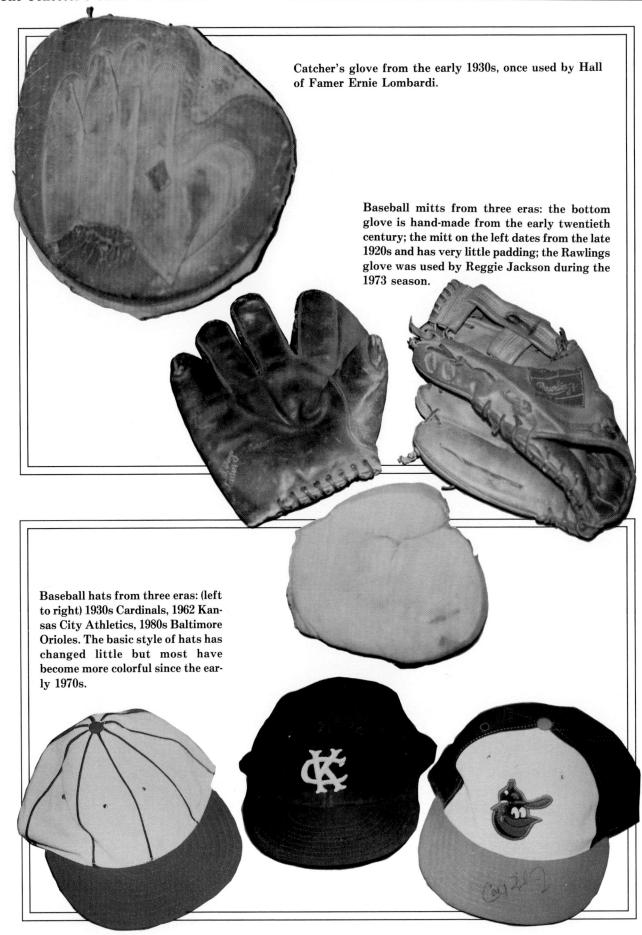

Catcher's glove from the early 1930s, once used by Hall of Famer Ernie Lombardi.

Baseball mitts from three eras: the bottom glove is hand-made from the early twentieth century; the mitt on the left dates from the late 1920s and has very little padding; the Rawlings glove was used by Reggie Jackson during the 1973 season.

Baseball hats from three eras: (left to right) 1930s Cardinals, 1962 Kansas City Athletics, 1980s Baltimore Orioles. The basic style of hats has changed little but most have become more colorful since the early 1970s.

"Game Used" Cracked Bats

Approximate Values from Contemporary Players

Bill Almon	$8.00-12.00	Steve Lake	$9.00-13.00
Dusty Baker	$13.00-20.00	Dave Lopes	$15.00-22.00
Don Baylor	$18.00-25.00	Bill Madlock	$45.00-55.00
Craig Bazzani	$5.00-7.00	Keith Moreland	$25.00-35.00
Dale Berra	$10.00-15.00	Omar Moreno	$9.00-12.00
Thad Bosley	$10.00-15.00	Al Oliver	$30.00-45.00
Scott Bradley	$12.00-18.00	Dave Parker	$40.00-55.00
Glenn Brummer	$8.00-10.00	Willie Randolph	$35.00-45.00
Jeff Burroughs	$8.00-12.00	Craig Reynolds	$10.00-15.00
Joe Carter	$16.00-18.00	Andre Robertson	$14.00-18.00
Henry Cotto	$8.00-10.00	Bill Russell	$20.00-25.00
Alvin Davis	$35.00-45.00	Billy Sample	$12.00-15.00
Bo Diaz	$15.00-18.00	Steve Sax	$30.00-40.00
Tim Foli	$9.00-12.00	Roy Smalley	$15.00-20.00
Bobby Grich	$18.00-25.00	Chris Speier	$12.00-15.00
Pedro Guerrero	$35.00-50.00	Andre Thornton	$25.00-30.00
Ron Hassey	$15.00-18.00	Bob Welch	$15.00-18.00
Burt Hooten	$15.00-18.00	Glenn Wilson	$25.00-35.00
Kent Hrbek	$50.00-65.00	Steve Yeager	$14.00-18.00
Jay Johnstone	$20.00-25.00	Joel Youngblood	$10.00-15.00

"Game Used" Bats

Approximate Values from Players in the Hall of Fame

Joe Cronin	$700.00-800.00	Bill Terry	$500.00-650.00
Napoleon Lajoie	$1,600.00-2,000.00	Honus Wagner	$1,100.00-1,500.00
Babe Ruth	$850.00-1,200.00	Rogers Hornsby	$900.00-1,000.00
Paul Waner	$300.00-450.00	Al Simmons	$400.00-575.00
George Kelly	$225.00-325.00	George Sisler	$400.00-525.00
Ed Roush	$200.00-325.00	Johnny Evers	$750.00-950.00
Ty Cobb	$1,500.00-2,000.00		

Dick Dobbins

(Dick Dobbins is a volunteer appraiser for the Baseball Hall of Fame and has been a collector of baseball memorabilia for over 30 years. He presently operates San Francisco Giants Memorabilia, the official clearing house for Giants equipment and memorabilia. Dobbins can be reached at P.O. Box 193, Alamo, CA 94507 or by phone at [415] 943-7384.)

I got my start as a serious uniform collector in about 1969 or 1970 when I was going through a flea market and came across somebody selling Kansas City Athletics jerseys for $7.00 apiece. Over the next year, I bought more than 200 of them, some of which I kept for my own collection and used others for trading. I started selling them, too, for the grand total of about $25 apiece. Well, those same jerseys now are rather premium items, selling for around $300 each. From that start it's been something that's grown enormously.

Another interesting early experience was when I visited the old ballpark of the Oakland Oaks of the Pacific Coast League, after the team had gone under and they were tearing the park down. I went down there on a nostalgia trip and as I was walking around, I kicked over a book which turned out to be a 1928 baseball guide. I followed along to a room that was about two feet deep in paper, and some of it turned out to be contracts of players from various years. I asked if it would be all right if I took some of the stuff and they said fine, so I walked out of there with four or five boxes full. I got Billy Martin's and Joe Gordon's first-ever contracts that they had signed. I even got the sale papers of the 1919 San Francisco Seals, and I don't know what that was doing in there.

Some of the baseball clubs have become more aware that selling their old equipment is a money-making venture. I had worked various projects for the San Francisco Giants over a series of years, and after about two-and-a-half years of my talking with them about selling uniforms, they gave me about 75 uniforms to sell, after the 1982 season. They were very skeptical and I don't think they expected much would come out of it, but I returned them an amount of money that "blew them away". To say they were flabbergasted is an understatement and from there on we've had a very positive relationship. After each season, they give me their uniforms to sell on consignment. This has satisfied many of their fans and has created excellent public relations for them.

In my sales, I've found there are a lot of frustrated Giants fans, most of them in New Jersey. I sell more uniforms to New Jersey than I do to California. The Giants have a better name associa-tion than a lot of other teams, better than the more successful Oakland A's right across the Bay.

The jerseys are originally the property of the ballclub and from time to time a player can ask for (and will receive) their jersey to keep after the season. The shoes and the gloves are property of the ballplayer, though. In New York Giants times, when the season ended, each Giants player received one uniform and that's been a pattern with other clubs. This, by the way, provides a great lead for collectors who might know a former player. I've talked to some ex-players who have literally thrown their uniforms away because they didn't feel they were of any interest or value to anybody else.

Teams differ in how many uniforms a player gets for use during the season. Normally a player is going to have two home and two road uniforms, but with superstars, they'll have a lot more. Reggie Jackson probably has more than any other because a lot of his are given away, a lot get put into charity auctions, and some are stolen as he goes from town to town. I would imagine a player like that is going through 20 uniforms a year. Pete Rose apparently had it in his 1985 contract that he would have the right to sell a multiple of uniforms. We know that for the game in which he set the hit record, Pete Rose wore three uniforms: one to keep for himself, one for the Reds ballclub, and one for the Hall of Fame.

A lot of teams have not made their uniforms publicly available, but that's a changing pattern. The New York Yankees knits, for example, are very difficult to come by. But the Yankees flannel uniforms are relatively easy to obtain - very often they're modified, but nevertheless they are quite common and quite desirable.

One of the negatives about collecting uniforms is that there's some faking of jerseys going on now, and you really have to be careful about what you buy. If you want to be confident about what you're getting, one suggestion is to choose a "common" player's uniform because you don't have the fraudulent activity occurring at that level. It's just not productive enough. It's the superstar players who will have their jerseys faked and you'd pay a premium for that uniform, whether it be real or fake.

Letters of authenticity are enormously helpful, and being able to look at the uniform is a good idea before buying. If there's been a name or number change on the jersey that makes it a superstar player's, I wouldn't touch it. Other modifications may be made to change names because of trades or for minor leaguers joining the big team. Those are more realistic changes that a lot of teams make - the Giants, A's, White Sox, Rangers, Indians and Tigers are among those that regularly modify their uniforms.

A big mistake a lot of people make is buying a uniform of a very good player with hopes of reselling it at a profit. Three years after that player has retired, unless he is a bona fide Hall of Famer, people will have forgotten about him and will have no interest in buying his uniform at a resale price that will make the original buyer money.

If you're a new collector I'd suggest you start small and work your way up. There are a couple of beginning strategies to take - you can try to come up with a representative style of each team or you can pick a favorite club (or clubs) and just specialize with them. Three good rules for being a safe buyer of a uniform are: 1) buy from reputable people; 2) feel free to ask for all the information about the background of the jersey; and 3) get an unqualified return guarantee.

I think that any collector of anything and certainly any sports fan, fantasizes about wanting to wear or to own a jersey of their favorite player. Buying these is one way of fulfilling a fantasy which can be done fairly cheaply today.

The "84" indicates the season in which the jersey was worn.

San Francisco Giants road jersey, worn by Johnnie LeMaster in the 1984 season.

The Giants are among a growing number of major league teams making their uniforms available to collectors on a yearly basis.

Chicago Cubs uniforms, such as this one once sported by reliever Donnie Moore, are in high demand.

This patch appeared on Chicago jerseys in the late 1970s.

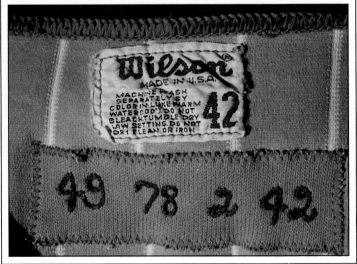

This tag indicates the player number (49), the season ('78), the set (2) and the size (42) of the jersey.

Cincinnati Reds windbreaker allegedly worn by slugging Dave Parker. Note the tag reveals that the jacket was worn during the 1984 season and is a size 48. The ink markings indicate that the windbreaker was used by number 39, Dave Parker.

Atlanta Braves bat boy jersey.

The "B.B." could stand for Billy Bruton or Bruce Benedict . . . but in reality, it stands for Bat Boy.

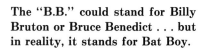

A New York Mets road jersey.

Doug Rader's jersey, worn during his tenure as manager of the Texas Rangers. Rangers gear is readily available to collectors.

Dave Bergman's autographed San Francisco Giants road jersey. Note that Bergman's number with the Giants was 16; his number with the Tigers is 14.

A patch commemorating twenty-five years in San Francisco, worn by Giants players during the 1982 campaign.

A San Francisco Giants bat boy jersey from the 1984 season. Bat boy and ball boy uniforms are typically priced in the $45.00-55.00 price range.

Mexican League knit jersey with vinyl lettering.

"Bush league" jersey from New England, circa 1890. Take special note of the collar, the lacing and the striped cap. This uniform is in remarkable condition after almost 100 years.

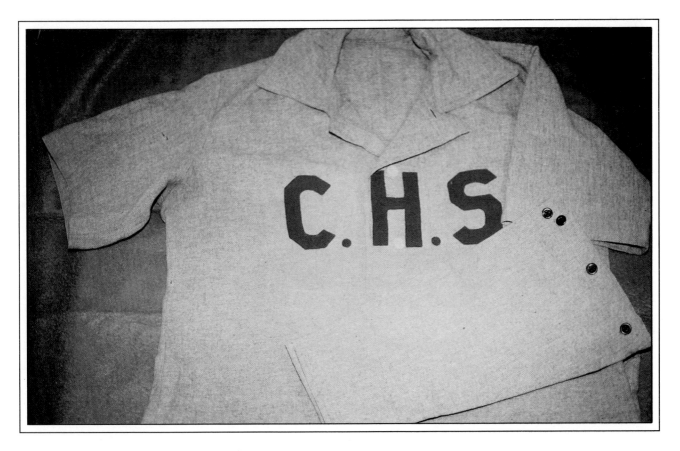

Jersey dated 1903 from Concord (N.H.) High School. This uniform is unique because of its removable sleeves.

Minor league jersey of unknown origin from the first quarter of the Twentieth Century.

Colorful uniform used in induction ceremonies at Cooperstown in 1939. Apparently each minor league in organized baseball was represented by a uniformed participant.

Sweater presented to New York Giants infielder Dick Bartell for making the major league All-America baseball team in 1937. A certificate signed by Babe Ruth accompanied the sweater. Bartell batted .306 in 158 games that season.

Sacramento Solons uniforms from the Pacific Coast League in 1939. The patch on the right sleeve celebrates the 100th anniversary of baseball.

A Sacramento Solons 1947 flannel road uniform.

St. Louis Cardinals home jersey, circa 1926, worn by Raymond "Jake" Flowers. Flowers had a ten year major league career and a lifetime batting mark of .256. Flowers died December 27, 1962.

St. Louis Cardinals road jersey of Hall of Famer Jay Hanna "Dizzy" Dean. The fact that the jersey has a number dates it from 1933 or later. Dean was elected to the Hall of Fame in 1953.

New York Yankees home flannel uniform from the 1951 season. Jersey has the rare 50th year American League anniversary patch on its left sleeve. Many Yankees flannel jerseys are found in less than desirable condition, because many were recycled through their minor league system. This Tommy Henrich uniform is an exception.

The Golden Anniversary patch on the Henrich jersey.

A St. Louis Browns uniform, worn by Ned Garver. Browns jerseys are scarce and expensive. Garver went 20-12 with the 1951 edition of the Brownies.

This uniform was sported by Hall of Famer Rogers Hornsby during his brief tour of duty as Browns skipper in 1952. Hornsby managed the Browns for 50 games that season and guided the Cincinnati Reds for 51 more games after leaving St. Louis.

54

Hornsby's name sewn into the collar of the jersey. In the 1950s it was common practice to sew the player's name into the collar rather than tagging the tail of the shirt as is done today.

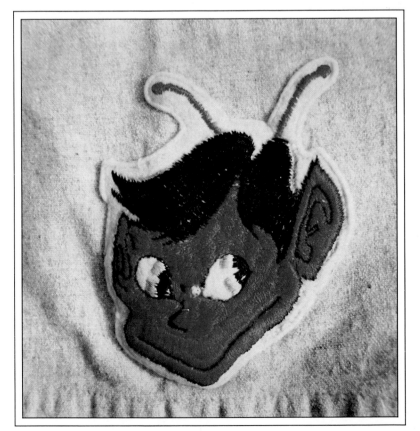

St. Louis Browns patch from a 1952 jersey.

Washington Senators jersey worn by catcher Ed Fitzgerald during the 1956 season when he rapped out 45 hits, including 8 doubles and 2 home runs, and had his career high batting average of .304.

Chicago White Sox home jersey used by Hall of Famer Luis Aparicio in the 1969 campaign. The patch on the left sleeve denotes the 100th anniversary of major league baseball.

San Francisco Seals jersey from the early 1930s, with embroidered lettering.

Cincinnati Reds vest-style jersey from the late-1960s. This one was worn in spring training by Johnny Bench. Bench began his career with the Reds by appearing in 26 games in 1967.

Home jersey of Forrest "Woody" Jensen during his 1937 season with the Pittsburgh Pirates.

Autographed Boston Braves "tomahawk"-style jersey from the 1940s worn by Warren Spahn, the winningest left-handed pitcher in baseball history.

Oakland A's vest-style jersey, worn in 1971 by Vida Blue. Charles O. Finley of the Kansas City/Oakland franchise was the first owner to introduce color into major league uniforms. The first knit jerseys were worn during the 1971 season. Vida Blue burst onto the scene in 1971, winning 24 games while losing only 8. Blue was the last American League MVP who was a switch-hitter.

This flannel jersey is valuable not because of the player who wore it, but because early Milwaukee Brewers uniforms are extremely hard to find. Bruce Brubaker was born in Harrisburg, Pennsylvania and had a lifetime big league earned run average of 13.50.

A Pete Rose Philadelphia Phillies jersey from the 1981 season. Jerseys of Hall of Famers and potential Hall of Famers are typically priced from $750 and higher. The tag on the Rose jersey indicates size 44 from the 1981 season, set number one.

Phillies uniform patch, worn during the 1984 season.

Embroidered front of St. Louis Cardinals road bat boy jersey.

St. Louis Cardinals road bat boy jersey.

Texas Rangers ball boy jersey.

The 100th anniversary of the Philadelphia franchise was celebrated with this Phillies patch worn during the 1983 season.

Top row, left to right: Cincinnati Reds patch from the mid-1950s; #19 - Dodgers patch commemorates the passing of "Junior" Gilliam; San Francisco Giants 25th anniversary patch; #40 - Astros patch commemorates the death of pitcher Don Wilson; 50th anniversary of the American League patch. Center section: Philadelphia Phillies 1976 patch; 1979 patch worn by a barnstorming team in Japan; Red Sox bicentennial patch from 1975; Montreal Expos 1976 Olympics patch. Bottom row: 1984 Dodgers Olympic patch; Los Angeles Dodgers 25th anniversary patch; 1969 patch to celebrate the 100th anniversary of major league baseball.

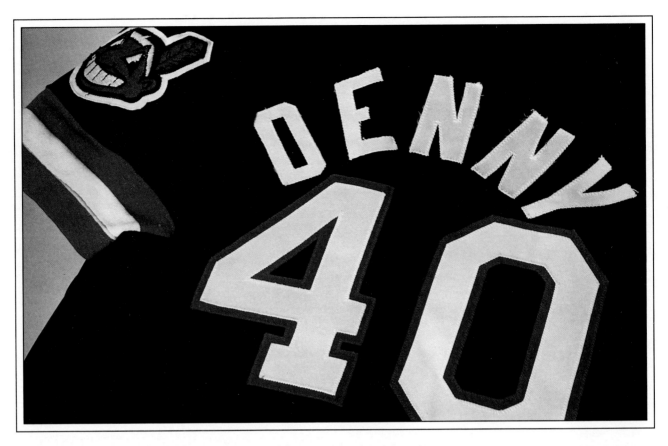

The Cleveland Indians are one of the few major league teams that sell their game-used hats, bats and jerseys directly to the public. The John Denny jersey was purchased from the Indians in 1983.

The script style logo of the Fresno Giants on a knit jersey.

Colorful home uniform of the California Angels from the early 1970s.

Complete with a halo, the state of California is shown on the sleeve of the Angels jerseys.

Example of the commemorative program handed out at each year's Hall of Fame induction ceremonies.

FIRST DAY OF ISSUE
JACKIE ROBINSON COMMEMORATIVE STAMP
THE BASEBALL HALL OF FAME
COOPERSTOWN, NEW YORK
AUGUST 2, 1982

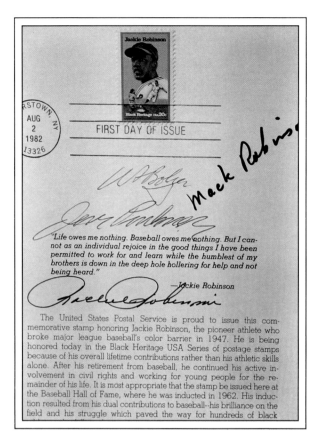

FIRST DAY OF ISSUE

"Life owes me nothing. Baseball owes me nothing. But I cannot as an individual rejoice in the good things I have been permitted to work for and learn while the humblest of my brothers is down in the deep hole hollering for help and not being heard."
—Jackie Robinson

The United States Postal Service is proud to issue this commemorative stamp honoring Jackie Robinson, the pioneer athlete who broke major league baseball's color barrier in 1947. He is being honored today in the Black Heritage USA Series of postage stamps because of his overall lifetime contributions rather than his athletic skills alone. After his retirement from baseball, he continued his active involvement in civil rights and working for young people for the remainder of his life. It is most appropriate that the stamp be issued here at the Baseball Hall of Fame, where he was inducted in 1962. His induction resulted from his dual contributions to baseball--his brilliance on the field and his struggle which paved the way for hundreds of black

Program given to spectators in attendance in Cooperstown on August 2, 1982 when the Jackie Robinson commemorative stamp was introduced.

The inside of this program has been signed by members of the Jackie Robinson family and by U.S. Postmaster General William Bolger.

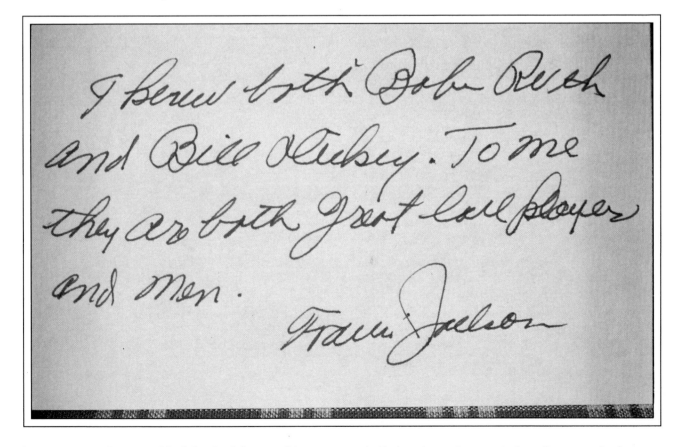

Some collectors have good luck in obtaining a written response to their autograph requests from former major leaguers. In addition to merely asking for a signature, a few short questions can bring some interesting responses.

One way of obtaining autographs is to get the signature on an 8 x 10 color photo, suitable for framing or displaying in plastic sheets. Hall of Famer Lou Brock is one of a few players to accumulate 50 steals and 20 home runs in the same season.

Hall of Famers Willie McCovey and Juan Marichal in their San Francisco Giants flannel-uniformed days. The autograph of Marichal is, primarily for geographic reasons, one of the more difficult to acquire.

WILLIE McCOVEY'S last at-bat July 6, 1980, Los Angeles

An autographed 11 x 14 picture of Willie McCovey's final time at bat in the big leagues.

Many experts believe getting signed 8 x 10s is preferable to having an autographed gum card of the player.

JOHN MARQUEZ Ind.

FELICITA A NUESTRO

JUAN MARICHAL

On the day that Juan Marichal was inducted into the Hall of Fame in 1983, many people from his native Dominican Republic were in attendance and distributed a quantity of these posters. After the ceremonies, several onlookers sought the autograph of a small, well-dressed gentleman in the crowd and were perplexed as to why he was signing the name, "Walter Alston", also a Hall inductee that day. Upon closer inspection, it becomes clear that the name is that of former Giants outfielder, "Mateo Alou".

Johnny Mize is one of the more congenial ex-big leaguers appearing at collector shows nationwide. The "Big Cat" cracked 359 career homers, including 51 in 1947.

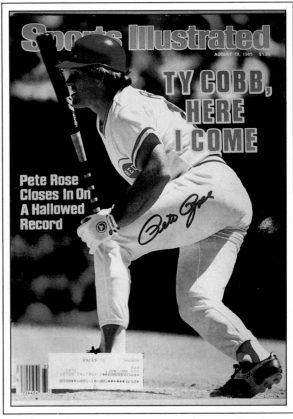

Pete Rose probably signed his name more times on more different pieces of baseball memorabilia in 1985 than most people will sign their names in their entire lifetime.

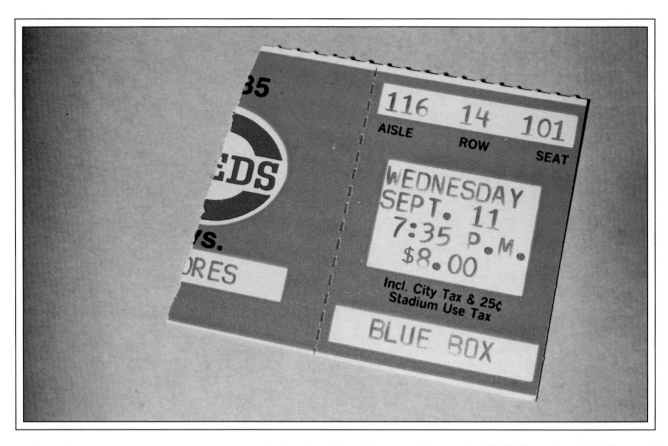

Ticket stub from the night Pete Rose eclipsed Ty Cobb's all-time hit record, September 11, 1985, against Eric Show and the San Diego Padres.

Collectors edition of The Cincinnati Enquirer the day after the Rose record was set. Reds fans everywhere, including Kevin Killian and Hank Nelson, were elated that Rose was able to break the Cobb mark at Riverfront Stadium.

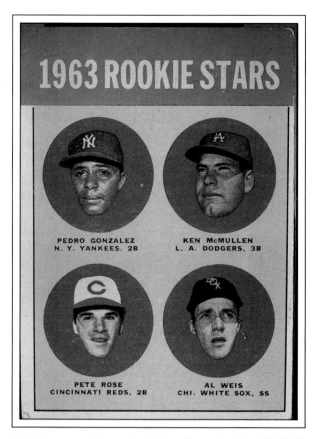

1963 Topps card featuring Pedro Gonzalez, Ken McMullen, and Al Weis. They amassed a total of 1,883 career hits. The player on the lower left bettered that total.

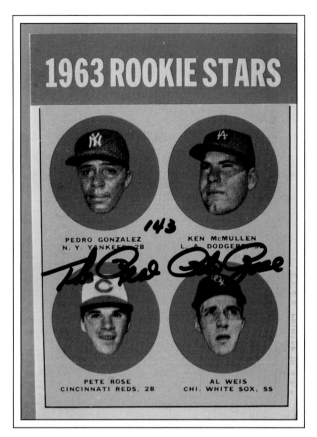

Counterfeit Pedro Gonzalez rookie gum card which has been autographed and numbered by "The Real Pete Rose".

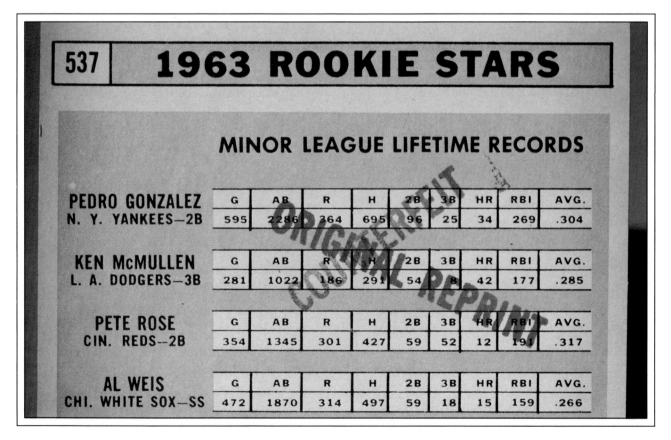

537	1963 ROOKIE STARS								

MINOR LEAGUE LIFETIME RECORDS

	G	AB	R	H	2B	3B	HR	RBI	AVG.
PEDRO GONZALEZ N. Y. YANKEES—2B	595	2286	364	695	96	25	34	269	.304
KEN McMULLEN L. A. DODGERS—3B	281	1022	186	291	54	8	42	177	.285
PETE ROSE CIN. REDS—2B	354	1345	301	427	59	52	12	191	.317
AL WEIS CHI. WHITE SOX—SS	472	1870	314	497	59	18	15	159	.266

The counterfeit Rose rookie cards were confiscated by the police and stamped on the back. As the prices of individual gum cards escalate, it will become economically feasible for additional counterfeits to find their way into the market.

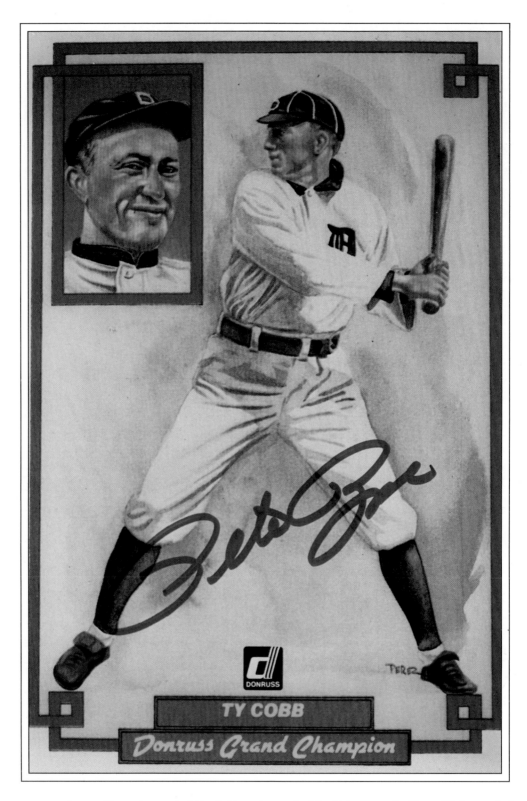

Donruss Grand Champion card of Ty Cobb, autographed by Pete Rose. As Barry Halper noted, with thought, some interesting combinations can be put together.

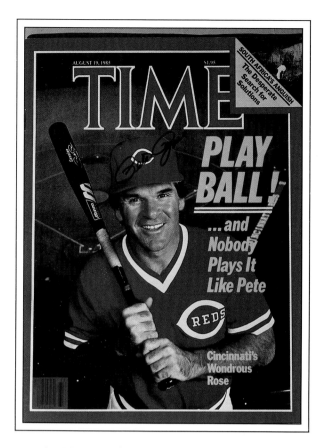

". . And Nobody Signs As Many As Pete", either.

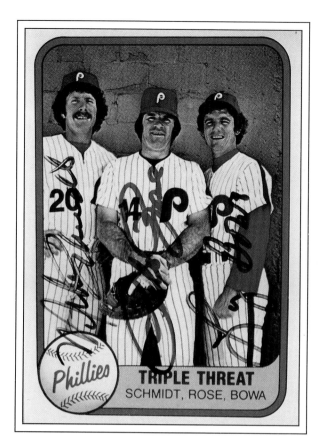

The signatures on this multiple player gum card were acquired over a two-year period. It would have been extremely difficult to catch Rose and Schmidt in the same setting.

Gateway Stamp Company of Florissant, Missouri first day cover which commemorates Pete Rose's 3,000th career base hit.

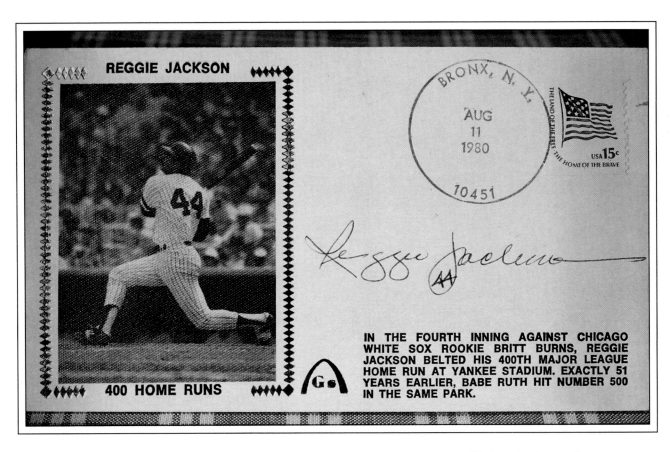

IN THE FOURTH INNING AGAINST CHICAGO WHITE SOX ROOKIE BRITT BURNS, REGGIE JACKSON BELTED HIS 400TH MAJOR LEAGUE HOME RUN AT YANKEE STADIUM. EXACTLY 51 YEARS EARLIER, BABE RUTH HIT NUMBER 500 IN THE SAME PARK.

Gateway cachet postmarked August 11, 1980 honoring Reggie Jackson's 400th major league homer.

Dugout lineup card of game between San Francisco and San Diego, April 10, 1985.

The Giants will sell nearly anything. Among the list would be their uniforms, lineup cards, George Foster, Jack Clark, and even Willie Mays.

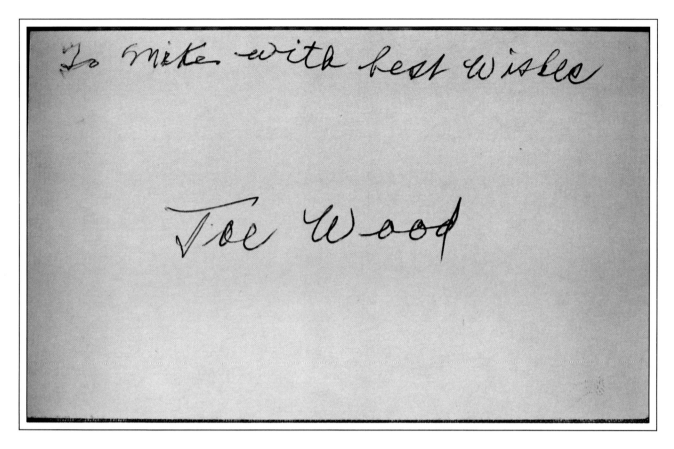

Personalized 3 x 5 card from "Smokey" Joe Wood, who had a 34-5 record as a 23-year-old pitcher for the Boston Red Sox in 1912. In the winter of 1986, *Sports Collectors Digest* featured an article about the availability of the largest sports collectible ever offered: Joe Wood's automobile.

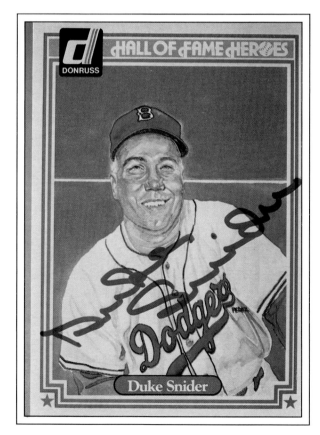

Edwin "Duke" Snider spent 18 years in the major leagues, including late stops with the Mets and the Giants. He tagged 407 career round trippers.

Bob Feller is a common sight at card shows and minor league ballparks across America.

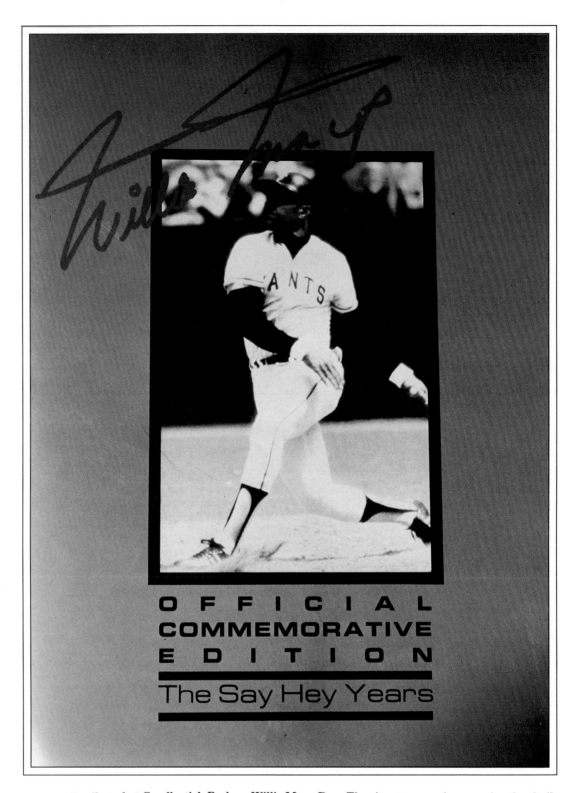

Program distributed at Candlestick Park on Willie Mays Day. The signature on the cover is a facsimile.

A difficult autograph (and interview) to obtain is that of future Hall of Famer Steve Carlton.

Puerto Rican-born Dick Perez, noted sports artist, featured on his own autographed Donruss Diamond King card.

Few little leaguers took the opportunity to learn the finer points of the game from these 95-cent records issued in 1973.

Donruss advertising brochure promoting the 1985 Lou Gehrig puzzle.

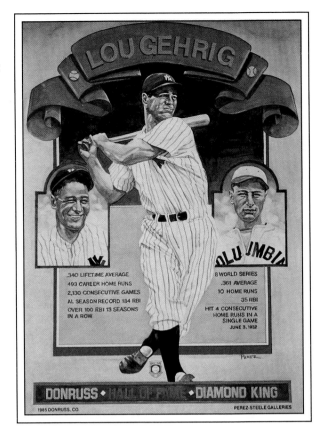

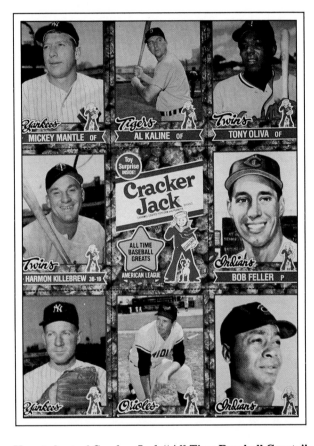

Uncut sheet of Cracker Jack "All-Time Baseball Greats". The cards were produced to celebrate the first Cracker Jack Classic old timers game in Washington, D.C.

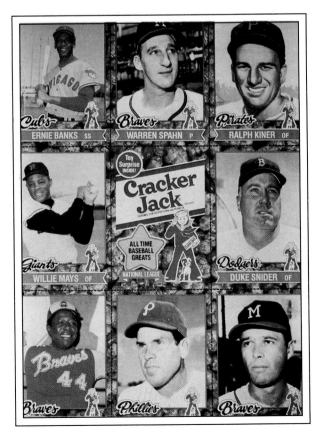

All of the players on the National League sheet are members of the Hall of Fame.

Pennant which celebrates the Giants league championship season of 1965. Unfortunately, no one told the Dodgers (the real pennant winners), who defeated Minnesota in the World Series in seven games. This "phantom" pennant also misspells the name of Hall of Fame Willie McCovey ((McCovery).

1984 All-Star press pin from San Francisco.

Whistle in the form of a baseball player, circa 1930s.

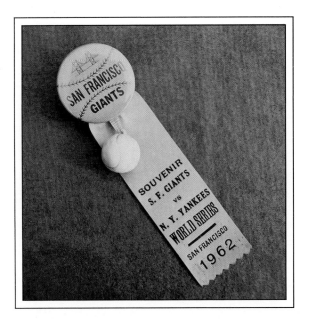

Souvenir button from the 1962 World Series in San Francisco.

Bleacher seats from New York's Yankee Stadium, made available to fans when the park was remodeled.

(At left) Croix de Candlestick pin given to all spectators at the 1984 All-Star Game in San Francisco. (At right) Keychain distributed to those witnessing Willie Mays's 600th career home run in San Francisco.

Ty Cobb's pipe.

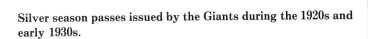

Silver season passes issued by the Giants during the 1920s and early 1930s.

Schedule of the 1935 Detroit Tigers issued by *The Detroit News*. They beat the Cubs in the 1935 Series. Road games were referred to as "abroad".

We would recommend the cereal, the chocolate-flavored drink and the energy bar, but would take a pass on the Fernando Valenzuela Mexican "Gum-Gum".

Bubble gum boxes with illustrations of baseball immortals.

Collectors will have to have plenty of room and/or plenty of money to acquire the large volume of printed matter made available each year through game programs, yearbooks, media guides and magazines.

In collecting printed material it is wise to specialize in a favorite topic - player biographies, fictional accounts, essays or histories are all moderately priced and readily available.

Bill Henderson

(Bill Henderson is the owner/operator of Bill Henderson's Cards, 1113 Columbus Circle, Janesville, WI 53545. His specialty is "common" baseball cards, the less expensive cards needed to fill out complete sets for card collectors.)

I look at baseball cards as things of beauty, in a way. There's a lot of color to them. You have a sport which you can follow as well as the cards of the individuals, containing their statistics. I'm in the "Baby Boomer" generation where there's a lot of nostalgia of the Fifties, and I think many people like to go back and collect some of this "beauty".

Since the cards are numbered, there's the desire in a lot of people to be able to complete something. You know how many are in a set and just like coins or stamps, you can figure out which elements are missing. But in the case of coins, there's only the silver and the coin itself to have. With baseball cards, we can actually meet the people who are pictured as well as go to the ballpark and see them play. I think the collecting of baseball cards and memorabilia will, conceivably, equal the collecting of coins and stamps in popularity. Who knows, it maybe even surpass them.

I was in the business of selling comic books for three or four years before I got into the baseball card world. I didn't care for the comic books, but I liked the idea of traveling and going to shows. My brother-in-law, Greg Onesch, picked up some cards and I told him that they looked like something I'd like to get involved with.

We went to a card show in Chicago in 1976 and that really made up my mind - I told Greg that we had to become dealers. After the experience I had in comic books, it was fairly easy to make the transition and within two or three months we had each obtained nearly 30,000 cards and were off to do our first card show. I didn't collect to begin with. I decided to be only a dealer and went out and aggressively sought to buy cards - by advertising in local, community newspapers.

From 1976 to 1980, collecting baseball cards probably experienced one of the biggest growth periods any hobby has ever seen. Each year we were seeing prices doubling and tripling, at a minimum. So 1976 is probably the baseball card equivalent to 1849 and the gold rush in California. I happened to get in at a very fortunate time.

I try to specialize in the sale of cards of a high quality condition, cards in "EX-Mint" or better. The first thing that dealers look at in determining card condition is the corners of the card. If the surface of a card is showing some wear, the corners are no doubt already gone. A card in "Mint" condition will have razor-sharp corners and the rest of the card would follow suit.

Cards classified in "EX-Mint" condition, which is the minimum condition I like to send out, allows for very small touches of wear on the corners - some visible sign that the corners have been handled. In "Excellent" condition there will be some corner rounding, and in "Very Good" condition there would be significant wear on the corners even though the card may be otherwise pleasing. Of the orders that I get, probably 75 per cent of the people specify that they want to have sharp condition cards and are willing to pay for it.

As an investment, I personally think getting baseball cards autographed is a poor approach. I find that for every 50 people who buy cards from me at a show, there are maybe one or two who collect autographed baseball cards. The majority of people I deal with are completing sets and would look at an autographed card as being defaced. I'd rather buy a $2 color picture and have the player autograph that . . . there will be less investment involved and probably a greater chance for appreciation.

I broke up my personal card collection a long time ago, so I don't have any real favorites. I do have some favorite people, though. The players I've met at shows who have shown kindness to both the dealers and the public. People like Enos Slaughter and Warren Spahn come to mind immediately. I enjoy the fellowship of the other people involved in the card hobby. That means more to me than the collecting of one particular set.

For beginning collectors I like the idea of buying current sets, setting them aside, and waiting for them to go up in price. You can buy a current set for about $18 and get around 800 cards. That's less than two-and-a-half cents apiece, but with inflation these cards will increase in value far more than the original $18. I'd also suggest a person new to collecting to buy what they like - if it is cards of star players you want, go after them. If you want to make your money last longer, buy top quality common cards and build up a large number of them. Everybody has different tastes in collecting . . . it's just important to have fun.

Hall of Fame Plaques

Yellow postcards with photographs of individual player's plaques from the Hall of Fame have been available since 1964. Prior to that date the original HOF postcards were black and white and were issued by Albertype (1936-early 1950s) and the Artvue Company (early 1950s-1963).

The cards are available from the gift shop at the Hall of Fame in Cooperstown, New York by the set (all members) or individually. They are **not** made in limited quantities like the Perez-Steele postcard series.

Signed plaques from the Albertype and Artvue periods of production are uncommon. Most collectors prefer the plaques to be "front signed" in Sharpie® rather than with a ball point pen.

Approximate Current Values of Selected Hall of Fame Plaques

Appling	$4.00-6.00	B. Leonard	$5.00-7.00
Berra	$8.00-11.00	Lopez	$6.00-8.00
Boudreau	$4.00-6.00	Mantle	$14.00-18.00
Chandler	$4.00-6.00	Mays	$10.00-12.00
Conlon	$4.00-6.00	Mize	$5.00-6.00
Coveleski	$10.00-12.00	Musial	$7.00-9.00
Feller	$4.00-6.00	Reese	$5.00-7.00
Ferrell	$6.00-8.00	Roberts	$5.00-7.00
Gehringer	$6.00-8.00	B. Robinson	$5.00-7.00
Greenberg	$9.00-12.00	F. Robinson	$7.00-9.00
Herman	$5.00-6.00	Roush	$5.00-7.00
Hubbell	$6.00-8.00	Sewell	$5.00-7.00
Irvin	$5.00-6.00	Slaughter	$6.00-7.00
T. Jackson	$6.00-8.00	Snider	$6.00-8.00
J. Johnson	$5.00-8.00	Spahn	$5.00-7.00
Kaline	$6.00-9.00	Terry	$6.00-8.00
Kell	$5.00-7.00	Wilhelm	$6.00-8.00
Kiner	$6.00-7.00	Wynn	$7.00-9.00
Koufax	$8.00-10.00	Williams	$14.00-18.00
Lemon	$6.00-8.00		

STANLEY FRANK MUSIAL
"THE MAN"

ST. LOUIS CARDINALS 1941-1963
HOLDS MANY NATIONAL LEAGUE RECORDS,
AMONG THEM: GAMES PLAYED 3026; AT
BAT 10972 TIMES; 3630 HITS; MOST RUNS
SCORED 1949; MOST RUNS BATTED IN 1951;
TOTAL BASES 6134. LED N.L. IN TOTAL
BASES 6 YEARS, SLUGGING PERCENTAGE
6 YEARS. MOST VALUABLE PLAYER 1943-
1946-1948. NAMED ON 12 ALL STAR TEAMS.
LIFETIME BATTING AVERAGE .331.

Autographed and corrected Hall of Fame plaque of Stan Musial. Notice on the card, Musial has corrected the error that has him appearing on only 12 All-Star teams. Musial was selected to 24.

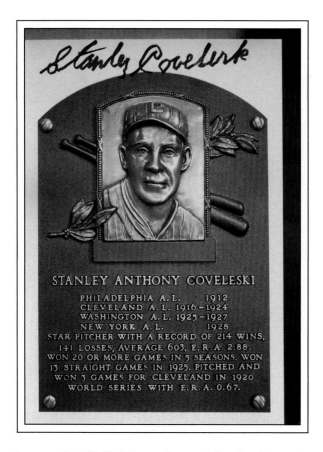

Autographed Hall of Fame plaque of Stanley Coveleski.

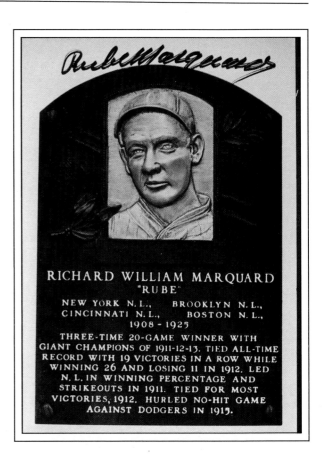

Autographed Hall of Fame plaque of Rube Marquard.

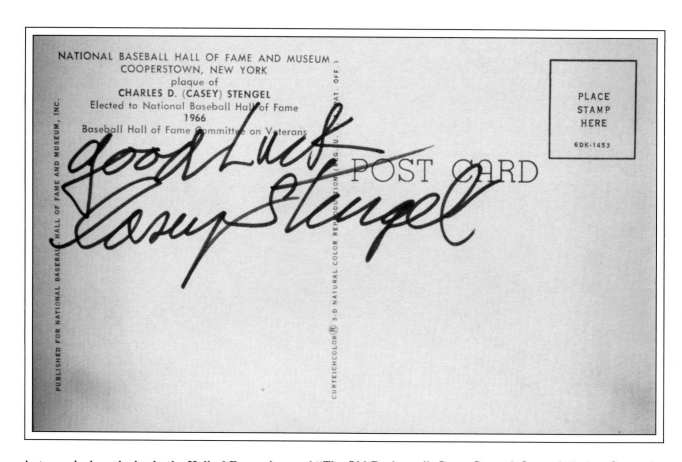

Autographed on the back, the Hall of Fame plaque of "The Old Professor", Casey Stengel. Stengel died on September 29, 1975.

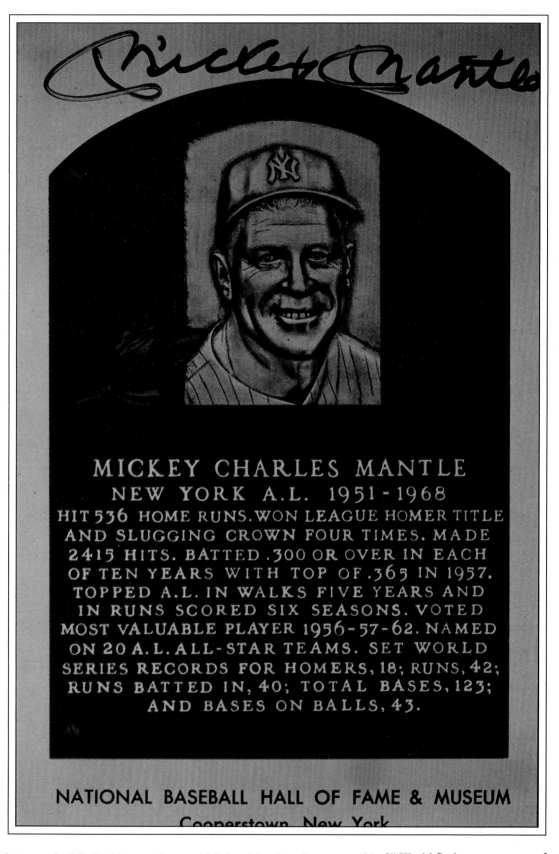

Autographed Hall of Fame plaque of Mickey Mantle, who appeared in 65 World Series games, second only to Yankees teammate Yogi Berra.

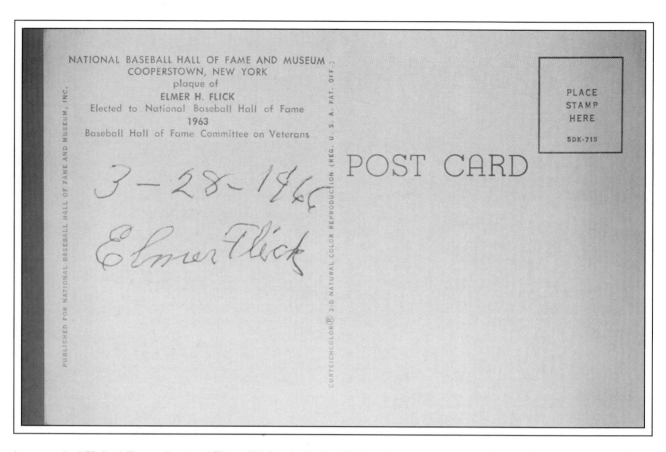

Autographed Hall of Fame plaque of Elmer Flick, who had a lifetime batting average of .315 in 13 major league seasons at the turn of the century.

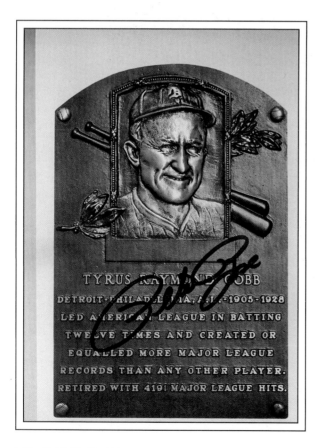

A Ty Cobb Hall of Fame plaque, signed by the man who surpassed Cobb as the game's leading hit-maker, Pete Rose.

Autographed Hall of Fame plaque of Burleigh Grimes, who won 25 games for Pittsburgh in 1928.

Bill Dickey's autographed Hall of Fame plaque. Dickey entered the Hall of Fame in 1954 along with Rabbit Maranville and Bill Terry.

Perez-Steele Postcards

The Perez-Steele Galleries of Ft. Washington, Pennsylvania initially issued a limited edition and numbered (10,000) set of water color paintings of members of the Hall of Fame in 1980. Periodically an additional series of postcards are made available to subscribers as new members are added to the Hall of Fame.

Collectors have tried with mixed success to secure signed cards from the players through the mail and at autograph sessions in Cooperstown or at local shows. Many of the cards can never be signed due to the death of the player before the date his card was available. Babe Ruth, Clark Griffith, Casey Stengel and Jackie Robinson are representative of

many players who were deceased prior to 1980. The signed cards that are considered "rare" are of players who were alive for only a relatively short time after the card was available. Players in this category would include Satchel Paige, Lloyd Waner, Earl Averill and Walter Alston.

James "Cool Papa" Bell, Roy Campanella and the late Red Ruffing were limited in their signings due to health-related difficulties.

Many of the Hall of Famers have been extremely gracious in signing their cards through the mail. Others sign only at shows and do not sign cards sent to them.

Approximate Values of Selected Perez-Steele Postcards

Aaron	$10.00-14.00	J. Johnson	$10.00-13.00
Aparicio	$20.00-25.00	Kaline	$10.00-13.00
Appling	$15.00-25.00	Kell	$8.00-12.00
Bell	$50.00-65.00	Kiner	$10.00-13.00
Berra	$10.00-15.00	Lemon	$10.00-13.00
Boudreau	$8.00-13.00	Lopez	$10.00-13.00
Brock	$9.00-13.00	Lyons	$30.00-40.00
Chandler	$10.00-15.00	Mathews	$10.00-14.00
Conlon	$10.00-15.00	Mays	$16.00-25.00
Dickey	$20.00-25.00	Mize	$10.00-13.00
Drysdale	$9.00-13.00	Musial	$13.00-18.00
Feller	$9.00-13.00	Reese	$10.00-14.00
Ferrell	$9.00-13.00	Roberts	$10.00-13.00
Ford	$12.00-16.00	B. Robinson	$10.00-14.00
Gehringer	$22.00-28.00	F. Robinson	$10.00-15.00
Gibson	$10.00-15.00	Roush	$16.00-25.00
Gomez	$10.00-15.00	Sewell	$12.00-16.00
Grimes	$30.00-45.00	Slaughter	$10.00-13.00
Herman	$10.00-13.00	Snider	$10.00-13.00
Hubbell	$25.00-35.00	Terry	$15.00-22.00
Irvin	$10.00-13.00	Wilhelm	$14.00-18.00
T. Jackson	$10.00-13.00	Williams	$35.00-50.00

Baseball signed by the only U.S. president ever to dress up and pretend he was Grover Cleveland Alexander.

Paper pennants purchased at Sportman's Park in St. Louis, c. mid - 1950s.

Child's catcher's mitt from the early 1930s. Uniforms, bats, and gloves made for children in the 1920 - 1950 period are still available and are usually underpriced. It is not unusual to find some interesting examples at flea markets or garage and tag sales.

"Say Hey Willie Mays" sunglasses from the early 1950s.

Willie Mays sunglasses from the early 1950s.

Bobbing head doll of Henry Aaron with the Brewers.

Bobbing head doll of Henry Aaron.

Ceramic bobbing head dolls.

Pennants from Coopeperstown, N.Y. It has been many years since a National Spelling Bee champion emerged from Coopeperstown.

Sandy Koufax coin issued by Topps in 1964. Koufax was #106 in a series of 120 All-Stars.

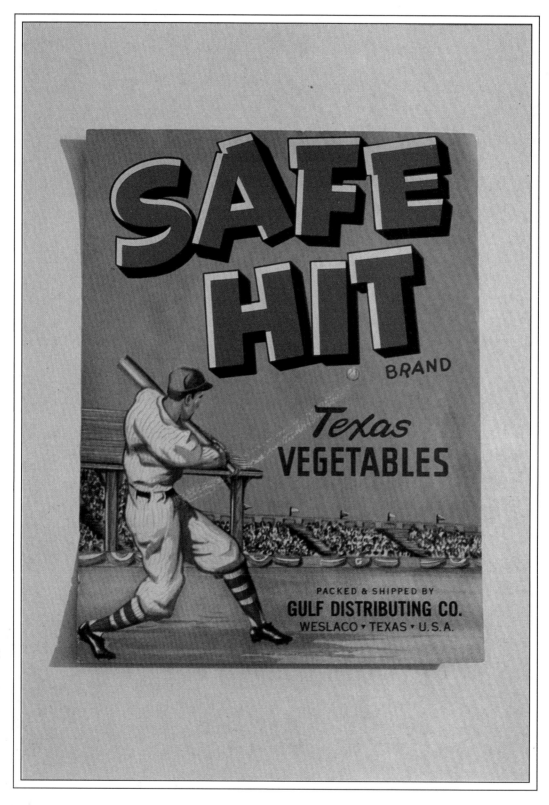

Unusual Safe Hit paper label (4″ x 7″) used on vegetable crates in the 1930s and 1940s.

Paper labels used on Perfecto Cigar boxes in the 1930s.

Autographed black and white photograph of former Memphis Chick and St. Louis Browns out-fielder Pete Gray.

Hartland Statues

The Hartland Plastics Company of Hartland, Wisconsin, manufactured eighteen different statues of major league baseball players between 1958 and 1963. Many were still available in small town dime stores and hobby shops for an additional four or five years.

The plastic statues sold for $3 to $5. A complete set of all eighteen players in excellent to mint condition would currently sell for $2,500-3,500.

In addition to the eighteen major league players, Hartland offered a 4″ minor leaguer and a 6″ Little Leaguer or bat boy. The Little Leaguer created some controversy when questions about the name and copyrights were raised by a youth baseball organization headquartered in Williamsport, Pennsylvania.

Condition is a critical factor in determining the value of a Hartland statue. If the plastic has yellowed over time or an arm or leg has been repaired or replaced, the value of a statue is diminished. Broken bats, faded or chipped paint, missing toe plates (bases) and a misplaced catcher's mask also are primary factors in the evaluation process.

Fourteen of the eighteen players who are depicted on the statues are in the Hall of Fame. Eleven of the players are holding baseball bats. There are still several suppliers who offer replacements for broken bats and Berra's catcher's mask.

Perhaps the two most valuable statues are of Dick Groat and Rocky Colavito. Their value is largely a function of an initial small demand and a limited distribution.

Listing of Hartland Statues and Approximate Values in Excellent to Mint Condition

Mickey Mantle* . . . $125.00-175.00	Nellie Fox . . . $125.00-200.00
Babe Ruth* . . . $125.00-175.00	Ernie Banks* . . . $125.00-200.00
Hank Aaron* . . . $125.00-160.00	Duke Snider* . . . $175.00-260.00
Eddie Mathews . . . $85.00-125.00	Don Drysdale . . . $200.00-250.00
Ted Williams* . . . $125.00-175.00	Rocky Colavito* . . . $300.00-400.00
Stan Musial* . . . $110.00-150.00	Luis Aparicio* . . . $200.00-250.00
Warren Spahn . . . $90.00-125.00	Harmon Killebrew* . . . $275.00-375.00
Yogi Berra . . . $115.00-170.00	Dick Groat* . . . $400.00-500.00
Willie Mays . . . $125.00-160.00	Roger Maris* . . . $175.00-275.00

*Posed with a bat

Musial and Berra both played on pennant winning teams but never faced each other in the Fall Classic.

Yogi Berra full figure Hartland statue with catcher's mask.

Few Berra Hartlands have survived with the original unattached masks.

St. Louis Cardinals great Stanley Frank Musial. Notice how even the batting posture has been accurately duplicated in this Hartland statue.

Musial, a minor league pitcher before injury forced a permanent move to the outfield, worked in a 1952 major league game on the mound for the Cardinals.

Hartland statue of Babe Ruth. The bat in Ruth's hand is a replacement.

The back of the Hartland Babe Ruth Figure.

Banks was selected as the National League MVP in 1958 and 1959. He hit 512 career home runs.

Banks played 1,125 games at shortstop, 1,259 at first base, 69 games at third, and patrolled the outfield in 23 contests, but was never involved in post-season play.

"The Commerce Comet" wore the number six when he first joined the Yankees, changing to number seven after Cliff "Tiger" Mapes was traded.

Mantle was the second American League switch-hitter to hit a home run from both sides of the plate in one game.

Movie Memorabilia

Reproduction New York Knights jersey and hat from perhaps the finest baseball movie ever made, "The Natural". At this writing, few of the jerseys actually worn in the film have been made available to collectors.

Programs, tickets, and uncut Roy Hobbs baseball gum cards.

Memorial Stadium in Buffalo was heavily populated with life-size cardboard figures during the filming of game sequences. This particular gentleman appears to be stunned by the pre-game ceremonies.

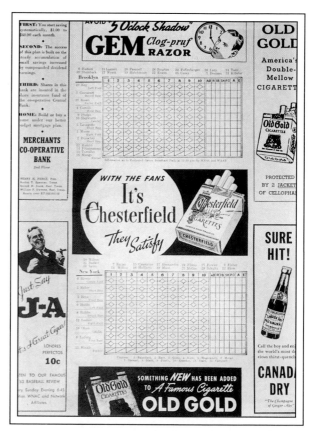

Scorecard of the ficticious Knights game against the Brooklyn Dodgers during the 1939 season.

The cardboard figures were stamped with the name of the film, the star, the location, and the year.

Robert Stephen Simon

(Robert Stephen Simon is a self-instructed painter who has been in the baseball collecting spotlight for about three years. Among the non-baseball subjects of the over 400 oil paintings he has done include football's Joe Namath and Doug Flutie, opera's Robert Merrill and film hero Sylvester Stallone. A catalogue of Simon's art is available by writing him at Robert Simon Studios, 43-70 Kissena Boulevard, Apartment 8-L, Flushing, New York, 11355.)

I began my sports artistry career by doing some paintings for the baseball hobby memorabilia business, the shows that go from coast to coast at which father, son, and fan alike can purchase autographed items of baseball collectibles. I used to do some of these shows myself, but now I keep myself in the studio because of my time schedule and I have people do shows for me in the New York area.

I was lucky to get great exposure, but it was some work I did in 1983 which catapulated me into recognition around the country. That's when I was able to do some paintings for George Steinbrenner. I did "50 Years of Yankees All-Stars" for Mr. Steinbrenner, and an original painting was presented on Old Timers Day to each Yankees legend that was present. I also did twelve pictures which are hanging permanently in the Yankee Club, a dining area for season ticket holders at Yankee Stadium.

Being from New York City, I concentrated in my early sports art work on the 1969 Mets, the early New York Giants at the Polo Grounds, the Yankees and the early Brooklyn Dodgers. I was quite surprised at the number of Brooklyn Dodgers fans all over the country. I got tremendous response in my mail orders for prints of the "Boys of Summer".

I also found a great deal of interest in nostalgic pieces (of Joe DiMaggio and Mickey Mantle) and of players that had already passed away (Lou Gehrig, Tony Lazzeri, Babe Ruth). One piece in partiuclar that I did featuring Hank Aaron and Babe Ruth, "Hank Eyes the Babe", was very successful. There have been five different paintings of Mantle that have been quite popular. My montage of Yankees stars of the last 50 years has Babe Ruth in the middle and was used in the Yankees program/scorebook with a larger version included as a pull-out in the Yankees yearbook.

My work has also been exhibited in the Baseball Hall of Fame. They commissioned me to do a piece on Nolan Ryan and Steve Carlton, who were at the time chasing the Walter Johnson strikeout record. All three pitchers were on the picture, which hung in Cooperstown all that summer and was one of my more interesting accomplishements.

When I'm doing these portraits, I never work off just one particular photo . . . it's always a combination of three or four, which makes it totally unique and lends an element of creativity. I have quite an extensive collection of sports photos, many of which come from old copies of *Sport Magazine* dating back to the Forties and Fifties, and I usually compose my paintings from a variety of these.

In my collectible work, besides selling my original paintings, I found I had to make my work available and affordable to any buyer. So, I decided to make reproduced prints (size 16 x 20 and 8 x 10) that could be sold by mail order, giving everybody a chance to buy my work at a relatively fair price.

I have done a lot in the last couple of years with Ron Guidry, Rickey Henderson, Dwight Gooden, Gary Carter and Don Mattingly, who is currently my hottest selling item. Also, I am now involved in doing higher priced, limited edition, fine art lithographs of sport, selling to the fine arts sports collectors around the country. These originals run anywhere from $1,500 up to about $5,000 and the framed lithographs sell for around $200.

Robert Stephen Simon has done much art work depicting New York Yankees players.

The inset shows Mays making his famous catch of the ball hit by Vic Wertz in the 1954 World Series, won by the Giants over Cleveland in four straight games.

Simon's 8 x 10 color prints are popularly priced and are excellent for autographing purposes.

"Hank Eyes The Babe" is one of Simon's favorite pieces.

Simon's portraits derive from a variety of photo sources

All-Star Game & World Series Programs

Prior to the 1974 World Series, each team involved in the classic produced a program to be sold at their home games. The 1974 program was the first to be a joint production of the teams and major league baseball. All of the programs evaluated below are assumed to be in excellent to mint condition.

World Series Programs

1967 at Red Sox	$55.00-70.00
1968 at Tigers	$75.00-85.00
at Cardinals	$75.00-85.00
1969 at Orioles	$40.00-45.00
at Mets	$50.00-60.00
1970 at Orioles	$40.00-45.00
at Reds	$60.00-70.00
1971 at Orioles	$40.00-45.00
at Pirates	$40.00-45.00
1972 at A's	$40.00-45.00
at Reds	$30.00-40.00
1973 at A's	$40.00-50.00
at Mets	$12.00-16.00
1974 Dodgers/A's	$17.00-19.00
1975 Red Sox/Reds	$12.00-14.00
1976 Yankees/Reds	$12.00-14.00
1977 Yankees/Dodgers	$12.00-14.00
1978 Yankees/Dodgers	$10.00-12.00
1979 Orioles/Pirates	$9.00-11.00
1980 Phillies/Royals	$7.00-9.00
1981 Yankees/Dodgers	$7.00-8.00
1982 Brewers/Cardinals	$7.00-9.00
1983 Phillies/Orioles	$5.00-7.00
1984 Padres/Tigers	$9.00-10.00
1985 Cardinals/Royals	$4.00-6.00

All Star Game Programs

1962 at Chicago	$60.00-70.00
1963 at Cleveland	$60.00-70.00
1964 at New York	$70.00-75.00
1965 at Minnesota	$50.00-60.00
1966 at St. Louis	$70.00-80.00
1967 at Anaheim	$85.00-90.00
1968 at Houston	$55.00-65.00
1969 at Washington	$55.00-65.00
1970 at Cincinnati	$70.00-80.00
1971 at Detroit	$60.00-70.00
1972 at Atlanta	$20.00-25.00
1973 at Kansas City	$65.00-75.00
1974 at Pittsburgh	$20.00-25.00
1975 at Milwaukee	$15.00-20.00
1976 at Philadelphia	$8.00-12.00
1977 at New York	$8.00-10.00
1978 at San Diego	$28.00-35.00
1979 at Seattle	$15.00-20.00
1980 at Los Angeles	$8.00-12.00

Mickey Mantle autographed baseball and a vintage glove.

Price Guide

NPA - No Price Available

Page 14-18
Items from the personal collection of Barry Halper are not priced because the vast majority are one-of-a-kind.

Page 19
Griffith ball $55.00-75.00
All-Star ball $6.00-8.00
Signed Olympic ball $45.00-50.00

Page 20
1942 ball $20.00-25.00
Wilhelm ball $65.00-75.00
Slaughter ball $65.00-75.00

Page 21
Aaron ball $20.00-25.00
Aaron card $20.00-75.00
Terry ball $65.00-75.00
Ferrell ball $65.00-75.00

Page 22
Ford ball $20.00-25.00
Robinson ball $100.00-135.00
Gibson ball $20.00-25.00

Page 23
Mantle ball $30.00-35.00
Baseball card $125.00-375.00
Magazine $10.00-12.00

Page 24
Mays's bat $65.00-95.00
Mays's ball $20.00-25.00
Bobbing head figure $15.00-25.00
Ripken ball $20.00-25.00
Smith ball $20.00-25.00

Page 25
Maris ball $100.00-125.00
Coleman ball $15.00-18.00
Yaz ball $75.00-95.00
PCL ball $15.00-18.00

Page 26
Rose ball $25.00-30.00
Cap $25.00-35.00
Davis bat $30.00-40.00
Sweat band $10.00-15.00
Davis ball $20.00-25.00
Gloves $15.00-20.00
Photo and cards . . . . NPA

Page 27
1948 ball $30.00-35.00
Minor league balls . . . . each $15.00-18.00
Old baseballs . . . . NPA

Page 30
Old bats . . . . NPA
Murphy bat $75.00-125.00

Page 31
Moreland bat $22.00-28.00
Minor league bat $12.00-15.00
LaPoint bat $15.00-18.00

Page 32
Brett bat $100.00-150.00

Page 33
Schmidt bat $100.00-150.00

Page 34
1980 W.S. bat $85.00-125.00

Page 35
Bat (unautographed) $15.00-20.00

Page 36
Hall of Fame bat $100.00-150.00

Page 37
Cruz bat $10.00-18.00
Davis bat $30.00-40.00

Page 38
Schmidt spikes $100.00-125.00
Cap $25.00-35.00
Sweatband $10.00-15.00
Glove $6.00-10.00

Page 39
Bergman glove $6.00-10.00
Schmidt glove $45.00-55.00

Page 40
Lombardi glove $300.00-400.00
Early gloves . . . . NPA
Reggie Jackson glove $350.00-550.00
1930 cap $100.00-150.00
1962 cap $75.00-125.00
Cal Ripkin cap $75.00-100.00

Page 43
LeMaster jersey $100.00-125.00

Page 44
Moore jersey $135.00-145.00

Page 45
Parker jacket $100.00-150.00
Bat boy jersey $45.00-55.00

Page 46
Mets jersey $100.00-125.00
Rangers jersey $100.00-125.00

Page 47
Bergman $100.00-125.00
Patch $10.00-15.00

Page 48
Bat boy jersey $45.00-55.00
Mexican jersey $200.00-225.00

Page 49
1890 jersey $500.00-600.00
CHS jersey $300.00-400.00

Page 50
Minor league jersey $400.00-500.00
Cooperstown jersey $600.00-800.00
Sweater $375.00-550.00

Page 51
1939 jersey $350.00-450.00
1947 jersey $325.00-400.00

Page 52
Flowers jersey $500.00-600.00
Dean jersey $2,500.00-4,000.00

Page 53
Yankee flannel $675.00-775.00

Page 54
Garver jersey $700.00-900.00
Hornsby jersey $1,500.00-2,500.00
Page 56
Senators jersey $400.00-600.00
Aparicio jersey $1,000.00-1,200.00
Page 57
Seales jersey $250.00-350.00
Bench jersey $900.00-1,300.00
Page 58
Jensen jersey $600.00-700.00
Spahn jersey $1,500.00-2,000.00
Page 59
Blue jersey $365.00-465.00
Brubaker jersey $350.00-400.00
Page 60
Rose jersey $1,000.00-1,400.00
Patch $5.00-8.00
Page 61
Cardinal bat boy jersey $45.00-55.00
Page 62
Texas ball boy jersey $45.00-55.00
Page 63
Phillies patch $5.00-8.00
Other patches . . . . NPA
Page 64
Denny jersey $120.00-140.00
Fresno jersey $55.00-65.00
Page 65
Angel jersey $100.00-125.00
Patch $5.00-8.00
Page 66
HOF program $12.00-14.00
Page 67
Robinson program $35.00-45.00
T. Jackson $8.00-10.00
Page 68
Brock picture $8.00-10.00
McCovey and Marichal $18.00-25.00
McCovey's last bat $18.00-25.00
Brooks Robinson $8.00-10.00
Page 69
Marichal poster $10.00-12.00
Mize picture $6.00-9.00
Rose magazine $20.00-25.00
Page 70
Ticket stub $6.00-8.00
Newspaper $5.00-7.00
Page 71
Original card $300.00-450.00
Signed card $30.00-40.00
Page 72
Donruss card $18.00-22.00
Page 73
Magazine $20.00-25.00
Phillie baseball card $18.00-22.00
First day cover $10.00-18.00
Page 74
First day cover $10.00-15.00
Lineup card $5.00-6.00
Page 75
Signed card $4.00-6.00
Snider card $5.00-7.00

Feller card $4.00-6.00
Page 76
Mays program $8.00-10.00
Page 77
Carlton card $8.00-10.00
Perez card $3.00-5.00
Records . . . . each $2.00-3.00
Page 78
Advertising brochure $1.00-2.00
Cracker Jack cards $6.00-9.00
Page 79
Pennant $20.00-24.00
Press pin $20.00-25.00
Whistle $15.00-30.00
Page 80
Button $12.00-20.00
Bleacher seat $75.00-125.00
Pin $12.00-20.00
Keychain $20.00-25.00
Ty Cobb pipe . . . . NPA
Season passes . . . . each $200.00-400.00
Page 81
Tiger schedule $12.00-20.00
Wheaties box $1.00-2.00
Rose can $10.00-12.00
Candy . . . . NPA
Gum boxes . . . . each $2.00-3.00
Page 82
Yearbooks and magazines $5.00-10.00
Books $3.00-10.00
Page 85
Plaque $7.00-9.00
Page 86
Coveleski plaque $10.00-12.00
Marquard plaque $10.00-12.00
Stengel plaque $12.00-15.00
Page 87
Mantle plaque $14.00-18.00
Page 88
Flick plaque $65.00-75.00
Cobb plaque $15.00-20.00
Grimes plaque $6.00-10.00
Page 89
Dickey plaque $10.00-14.00
Page 91
Reagan $100.00-200.00
Page 92
Pennants . . . . each $5.00
Page 93
Child's glove $15.00-20.00
Page 94
Sunglasses $65.00-85.00
Page 96
Aaron doll $15.00-25.00
Page 98
Cleveland & Baltimore dolls $14.00-18.00
Page 99
Pennants $2.00-3.00
Koufax coin $8.00-12.00
Page 100
Safe hit label $1.00-3.00
Page 101
Cigar labels $2.00-3.00

Page 102
    Gray picture $10.00-15.00
Page 105
    Berra $115.00-170.00
Page 107
    Musial $110.00-150.00
Page 109
    Ruth $125.00-175.00
Page 111
    Banks $125.00-200.00
Page 113
    Mantle $125.00-175.00
Page 115
    Knights jersey $100.00-125.00

    Cap $15.00-25.00
    Phillies program $12.00-20.00
    Dodger program $50.00-75.00
    Ticket $12.00-15.00
    Cards $15.00-20.00
Page 116
    Cardboard figures . . . . each $35.00-45.00
    Scorecard $20.00-25.00
Page 118-122
    Simon prints . . . . each $5.00-12.00
Page 124
    Mantle ball $30.00-35.00
    Glove $15.00-20.00

On the Cover:
Cap - $15.00
Program - $6.00-10.00

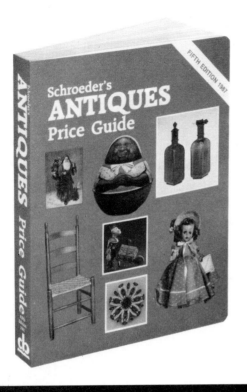